LEARNING MUSIC
GarageBand® on the iPad

FLOYD RICHMOND

The Essential Classroom Guide to
Music Production, Performance, and Education
with iOS Devices

DOWNLOAD FREE CORRELATING MEDIA

Visit **alfred.com/LearningGarageBand** to download free correlating videos and files for *Learning Music with GarageBand on the iPad*. The website also provides periodic updates to keep this book current with the latest info on audio technology. Simply visit **alfred.com/LearningGarageBand**, and sign in to access files and receive e-mail alerts when new material is added.

Alfred Music
P.O. Box 10003
Van Nuys, CA 91410-0003
alfred.com

Copyright © MMXV by Alfred Music
All rights reserved. Printed in USA.

GarageBand and iPad are registered trademarks of Apple Inc., registered in the U.S. and other countries. All other trademarks are the property of their respective owners.

Produced in association with Lawson Music Media, Inc., Nashville, TN
www.lawsonmusicmedia.com

No part of this book shall be reproduced, arranged, adapted, recorded, publicly performed, stored in a retrieval system, or transmitted by any means without written permission from the publisher. In order to comply with copyright laws, please apply for such written permission and/or license by contacting the publisher at alfred.com/permissions.

ISBN-10: 1-4706-1968-7 (Book & Media)
ISBN-13: 978-1-4706-1968-8 (Book & Media)

Contents

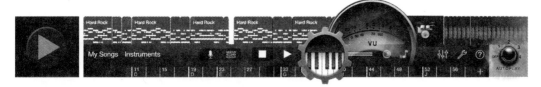

Introduction: GarageBand for iOS Devices

When Apple introduced GarageBand, music teachers everywhere took notice. Not only had Apple developed a great tool for recording music, it had introduced a collection of tools that encouraged creativity and composition, two of the most significant goals of music educators. Furthermore, it did so with a simple interface that was approachable for students of all ages and levels of musical experience. Regardless of the depth of their previous musical training, students and teachers could compose music at higher levels than ever before.

Traditionally, one of the biggest frustrations for students has been the time required to master foundational concepts before they could produce musically satisfying results. With the advent of GarageBand, students can connect their innate musicianship to a final product in a way that engages their imaginations and removes many previous obstacles.

Why iOS?

The use of GarageBand on iOS devices is growing. Increasingly, school districts are providing students with iPads, and as of this writing, GarageBand iOS is free although, some in-app purchases may be required to add the full set of instruments.

On a general level, iPad and tablet computing is likely to continue to grow. iPads make the Internet and email easily accessible, and users can carry literally thousands of pounds of books on a single device. The benefit of having an entire collection of textbooks on a device that weighs about a pound should be apparent to anyone who has ever struggled to carry a large bookbag. Furthermore, Internet browsing and email represent a large percentage of the kinds of computing people do, and especially what is required of most students in the classroom. Even at their current level of development (and without considering GarageBand), iPads provide the majority of general computing services needed by students.

On a musical level, the number of features of GarageBand for iOS is likely to increase, as is the strength of other multimedia programs such as iMovie, which is already a capable iOS program that integrates well with GarageBand. Also, the number of hardware peripherals that support music production is increasing, as is the number of apps that can supplement GarageBand and interact with it through interapplication communications.

iPads are now, and probably always will be, less capable than their laptop and desktop cousins. The level of performance is not likely to be a significant issue though. There has been near-universal acceptance of laptops, even though more powerful desktop computers cost less. People are willing to work with the limitations of laptops because of their relative power and portability, and the same is likely to be true with iPads and other tablet devices. With continuing advances in the power and function of iPads and with their significantly lower cost, they will likely replace laptops one day. Already, notable training programs, such as Penn State's medical school, provide incoming students with only a tablet device upon entry.

GarageBand for iOS and Mac

Apple introduced GarageBand for Mac (laptops and desktops) in 2004 and followed that with GarageBand for iOS in 2011. Although GarageBand for iOS is missing some of the features of GarageBand for Mac, it also has some features not found in the desktop version. For example, GarageBand for iOS allows you to automate the accompaniment for specific chords. GarageBand for Mac requires you to manually record specific chord progressions or use (or edit) the chord progressions found in its MIDI loops.

GarageBand for iOS also has a drum machine interface for creating automatic drumset parts that is based on artificial intelligence and on input from the composer, who can specify how complex and how loud the parts should be. This interface is also found on high-level digital audio programs, such as Logic, but it is not found in GarageBand for Mac.

To be sure, GarageBand for Mac can do some things that GarageBand for iOS cannot. For example, GarageBand features pitch correction, rhythmic correction of digital audio, notation view, and MIDI editing, as well as a greater variety of digital audio effects and a larger library of loops and instruments. For a more detailed comparison of GarageBand for Mac and GarageBand for iOS, see Appendix A: Features of GarageBand for Mac and GarageBand for iOS.

However, there is nothing that prevents starting a project on GarageBand for iOS and later sending it to GarageBand for Mac, to take advantage of those additional editing features. If neither GarageBand for iOS nor GarageBand for Mac provides enough editing features, you can open GarageBand songs and projects directly in Apple's professional-level digital audio program, Logic Pro X.

While it is possible to start a project on an iOS device and then to take it to a more powerful laptop or desktop computer for editing, Apple's official position is that, at this time, you cannot move projects edited in GarageBand for Mac or in Logic back to GarageBand for iOS. This is logical, because edits made on a program with additional instruments and features could not be executed on GarageBand for iOS. However, if you need to take music back, you can work around this limitation to some degree by exporting individual tracks from the high-end programs and reimporting them into GarageBand for iOS, or by mixing down tracks that were changed on the more powerful programs and then exporting and reimporting them.

A good example of why you might need to do this would be in the case of vocals and backgrounds that were recorded on an iPad. You might need to align the attacks of each lyric. In GarageBand for iOS, this is a tedious manual process. In GarageBand for Mac or in Logic Pro X, you can do it automatically. You may complete the edited project on the Mac, but it may make sense—especially for portability or for field work—to send those tracks back to GarageBand for iOS. The specific process for doing this will be described in Chapters 1 and 8.

Who Uses GarageBand for iOS?

GarageBand is a music-making and recording program that is useful for musicians at many levels. Beginners can reach new heights in their songwriting and musically-creative activities by using GarageBand's building blocks (*loops*). Performers can explore new musical ideas and execute them on GarageBand's numerous virtual instruments. Musicians, producers, and bands can create demo songs or record a track before the idea is gone. Experienced musicians and professionals can start projects on their iPads and can often complete them with nothing more. If they run into limitations in GarageBand for iOS, they can transfer their work to a professional-level application, such as Logic Pro or Pro Tools, without loss of quality.

What Does GarageBand Do?

GarageBand for iOS permits those using it to complete a number of musical tasks including:

- Playing and recording an extensive collection of outstanding, built-in virtual instruments

- Creating or enhancing music using prerecorded building blocks called loops

- Recording music through a microphone to multiple tracks

- Importing previously recorded digital audio tracks

- Enhancing music through the use of numerous special effects, such as reverb, equalization, compression, and rhythmic correction

- Editing digital audio tracks through copy-and-paste, duplication, looping, and numerous other effects

- Recording music played on external MIDI devices (such as keyboards, guitars, MIDI violins, electronic drums, and electronic wind controllers)

- Enhancing previously recorded MIDI tracks using effects such as reverb and unique MIDI effects, such as instrument substitution

- Editing MIDI tracks through note-by-note pitch correction, even of harmonic material, using a piano-roll editing system

- Performing rhythmic correction (quantizing attacks and/or durations or adjusting durations, velocity correction, and editing of articulations)

What's So Great About GarageBand?

When it was first released, an initial advantage of GarageBand over existing music-production programs was that Apple distributed GarageBand with every Mac at no additional cost. At first, they distributed it on iOS devices for $4.95, before making the basic app free in 2013. Every Mac since GarageBand was introduced has come with the software, and users of machines made before it was introduced could add it at low cost if the machine was sufficiently powerful.

GarageBand is free on the App Store for compatible devices; additional GarageBand instruments and sounds are available with an in-app purchase. Downloading apps requires an Apple ID.

Another great innovation of GarageBand is its ease of use. Apple had worked extensively on making the program accessible, and the result is that the tasks accomplished by most music-production programs are much easier in GarageBand.

Also high on the list of GarageBand's unique innovations was an extensive collection of musical building blocks called loops. Although there were already loop-based programs, there was nothing on the scale of GarageBand. Its number and quality of loops far exceeded anything previously available. Composers could use the loops to write music, and producers could use them to create recordings. Again, GarageBand's ease of use far surpassed anything previously available.

GarageBand also came bundled with an extensive collection of instruments that even today dwarf many high-end production programs. It's not uncommon for professional-level DAWs (digital audio workstations) to come with only a few instruments—for example, a keyboard with just a few sounds, a sampler, and a percussion instrument with just a few sounds.

Because it is so approachable, GarageBand has often served as an entry point for people to learn the basics of recording before they move on to more sophisticated DAWs, such as Pro Tools, Logic, Digital Performer, Cubase, and many others. Because GarageBand is so capable, however, many people find that it meets all their needs.

System Specs

The examples in this book are written using GarageBand 2.0 for iOS 7. Of course, those using earlier and later versions of GarageBand will notice some differences, but the conceptual framework of the program will be very similar. Following is some compatibility information for GarageBand 2.0 and iOS 7. See _www.apple.com/ios/garageband_ for complete details.

GarageBand 2.0 compatibility:

- Requires iOS 7.0 or later

- Compatible with iPhone, iPad, and iPod Touch

- Optimized for iPhone 5

- Thirty-two tracks available on iOS devices with the A7 chip. Sixteen tracks available on iPhone 5c, iPhone 5, iPhone 4s, iPad (3rd and 4th generations), iPad 2, iPad Mini, and iPod Touch (5th generation)

- Using third-party musical instruments requires devices made for iPhone, iPad, and iPod Touch

Installing GarageBand

If GarageBand is not already installed on your iOS device, you will need to add it. If GarageBand *is* installed, there will be a GarageBand icon on one of the iOS device screens, as shown in Figure i.1.

Figure i.1

If you don't see a GarageBand icon on the desktop, then from your iOS device, launch the App Store and search for Apple GarageBand, as shown in Figures i.2 and i.3.

Figure i.2

A number of supporting GarageBand projects and apps are available. Apple manufactures GarageBand, whereas the numerous tutorials and supporting applications are generally published by third parties. For now, skip those and download GarageBand.

The button in Figure i.4 labeled Open will read Install on devices without GarageBand. Click it to continue.

You'll need an Apple account with a unique ID and password. Log in, download or purchase the app, and install it on your iOS device. Then, let the songwriting and composing begin. You can log in to your account from any iOS device and install GarageBand to that device.

You can use giftcards from the iTunes Store to purchase GarageBand's instruments, but you must redeem the giftcard before you start your purchase. To do so:

Figure i.3

1. Tap iTunes Store, App Store, or iBooks Store on your iOS device.

2. Scroll to the bottom of the Featured section and tap Redeem.

See this Apple Support Document for more information:

www.apple.com/support/itunes/cards-codes/

Resources Accompanying This Book

This book's Table of Contents lists songs found on the accompanying media (downloadable from *www.alfred.com/LearningGarageBand*). These files will be one of two types:

Figure i.4

- **Audio recordings (.wav audio files).** Just listen and enjoy. You can add these to your iTunes Library.

- **GarageBand files.** All GarageBand (.band) files distributed with this book can be opened on any iOS device running GarageBand 2.0. You can also open the files using GarageBand or Logic Pro for Mac on a laptop or desktop computer.

Chapters 1 and 8 of this book describe transferring files from laptop and desktop computers to your iPad.

The pictures below show an iPad and the location of each of its controls and input and output connectors. In conjunction with the iPad's touch screen, these will be used extensively.

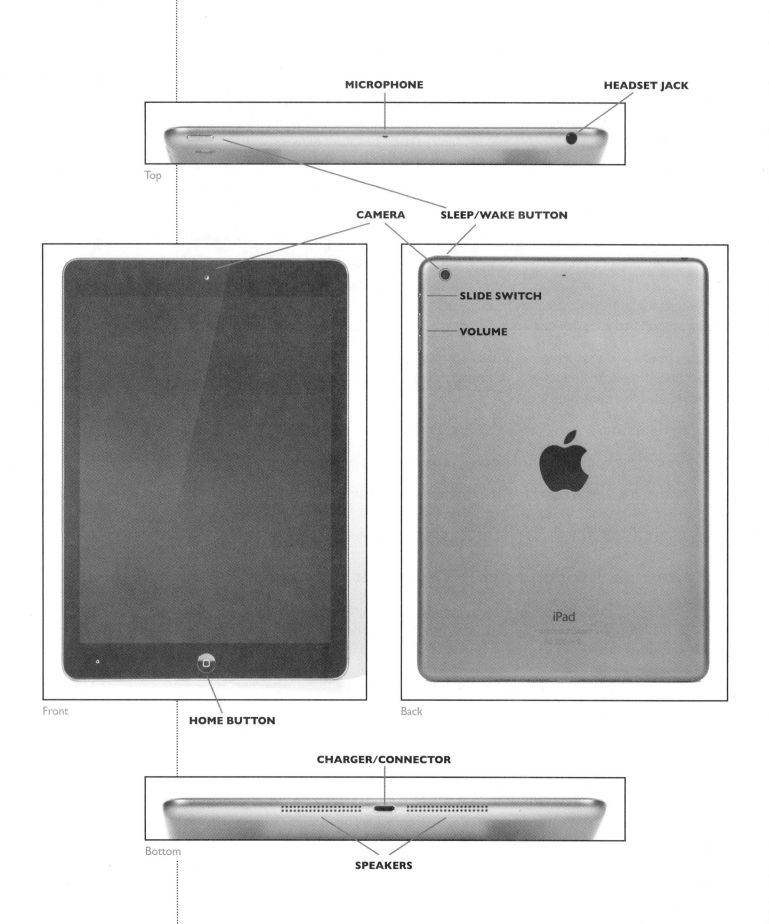

MICROPHONE   HEADSET JACK

Top

CAMERA   SLEEP/WAKE BUTTON

SLIDE SWITCH

VOLUME

iPad

Front   Back

HOME BUTTON

CHARGER/CONNECTOR

Bottom

SPEAKERS

Chapter 1: Quickstart 1—Playing a Demo Song, Recording a Vocal Background Track, and Replacing the Lead Vocals

When you launch GarageBand, one of several possible screens will appear, depending on whether it's the first time GarageBand has run or what you were last editing in the program. This feature that enables the program to return to the last thing you were editing is a convenience—if you switch to another program or take a phone call, or if GarageBand crashes or the battery runs down (rare occurrences), all recent edits will be saved and you'll be able to resume working where you stopped.

This list of possible views is complete as of this writing, but new versions of GarageBand may introduce others.

The **Song List View** in Figure 1.1 shows the projects you've created in GarageBand for iOS on your iPad. Click on a project to open it. You can sort the songs by date or by name by clicking on the appropriate button at the top of the screen. Click the + button to create new songs. Use the Select button to duplicate or delete songs, send them to the computer, or share them on social networks.

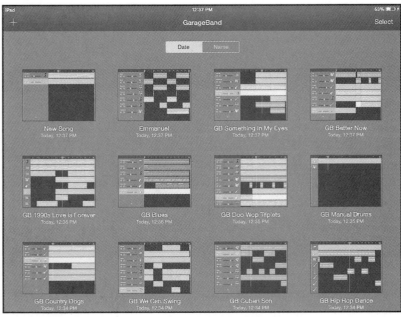

Figure 1.1 Song list.

The **Track View** in Figure 1.2 has a menu bar across the top, a ruler showing measure numbers, and tracks that represent each instrument or voice in the song. Each track has controls to the left and data to the right.

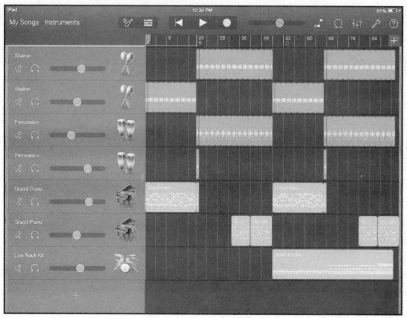

Figure 1.2 Track view.

The **MIDI Editor View** shown in Figure 1.3 lets you edit specific notes in MIDI tracks (tracks recorded for virtual instruments). Each "bubble" represents a note, and you can adjust or customize the many properties of each note from this screen.

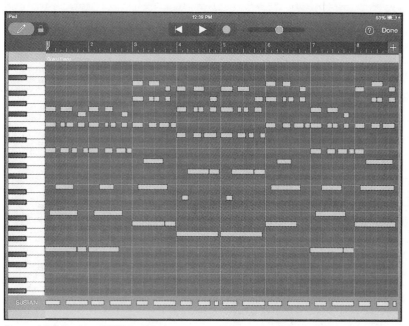

Figure 1.3 Edit view (MIDI bubbles).

The **Instrument Selection View** shown in Figure 1.4 lets you select an instrument to add to the song. Swipe left or right to see the various instruments, and tap on one to select it.

Figure 1.4 Instrument selection.

The **Instrument Settings and Performance View** shown in Figure 1.5 allows you to change instruments—for example, you can choose whether you want to use piano or electric piano. After you select an instrument, you can use it to perform and record in this view.

Figure 1.5 Instrument settings and performance.

The **Menu View** shown in Figure 1.6 lets you select various program and document options and perform various types of editing. GarageBand has numerous menus, which you can open by tapping a tool or submenu and close by setting the values and tapping elsewhere.

Figure 1.6 Menu view.

You will eventually find each of these views useful, but for now, let's navigate to the Song List View.

If you are on the song list, great. If not, then check the top-left corner for a menu option that says My Songs and tap it. If there is no menu that says My Songs, then look for one that says Done or Back and tap it, and then tap My Songs.

Note: If there is an open menu, close it first. (To close an open menu, tap on something other than the menu.)

When you're on the song list, the screen should look like Figure 1.1 (although perhaps with fewer songs).

The GarageBand Song List

iOS device uses a file system that is very different from other computers. It is common for each iOS app to provide a list of documents it has created or that are available for editing. The song list is that place for GarageBand.

The lessons in this book utilize GarageBand files that can be downloaded from _www.alfred.com/LearningGarageBand_. Follow the instructions on the next page to transfer those files to your iOS device.

HOW TO TRANSFER GARAGEBAND FILES TO YOUR IOS DEVICE

1. From a Mac, navigate to *www.alfred.com/LearningGarageBand*

2. Navigate until you see the file called Celebration.zip

3. Right-click the file and download it to your computer

4. If the browser does not automatically do so, double-click the downloaded file to expand it

5. Launch iTunes

6. Connect your iOS device to your computer

7. Click on your iOS device's icon in iTunes

8. Click on the Apps tab

9. Scroll down to the File-Sharing section

10. Click on the GarageBand icon

11. Drag the downloaded song into the GarageBand window (be certain to use the expanded version, and not the .zip file)

12. Open GarageBand on the iOS device and navigate to the Song List view

13. Click the + sign for a new song and choose Copy from iTunes File Sharing

14. Find the downloaded song and double-tap it

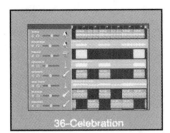

Figure 1.7 View of Celebration

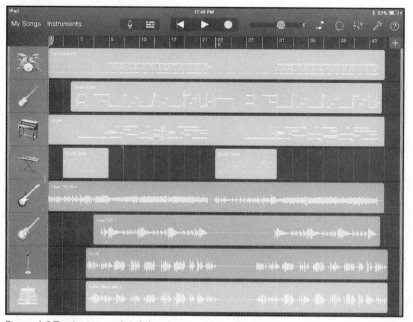

Figure 1.8 Track view with left-hand controls condensed.

GarageBand Track View

We did not tour all of the song list options, but the best Quickstart process will have us using several views. We'll revisit the song list later.

The Track view shows the structure of the song. On the far left is a list of instruments representing each performer in the ensemble. To the right of those icons is data representing each performer's individual recording. Across the top of the screen are the program's menus and controls, as shown in Figure 1.9.

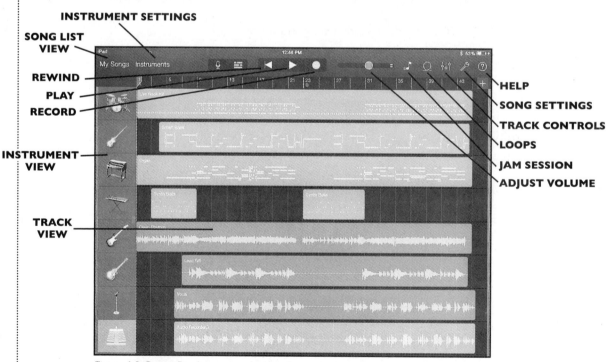

Figure 1.9 GarageBand menus and controls.

In the center is the transport, with rewind, play, and record buttons visible, as
shown in Figure 1.10.

Figure 1.10 GarageBand's
transport controls.

The menu button on the far right of the screen, shown in Figure 1.11, deserves
special mention. It is shaped like a question mark and is the Help button.

Figure 1.11 GarageBand
Help button.

This chapter and most that follow will include lists of functions. Most are
intuitive or easy to remember; however, if you forget or can't quickly find
something in the book, click the Help button to show a list of commands. This
convenient reference is available from most GarageBand screens. See Figure 1.12.

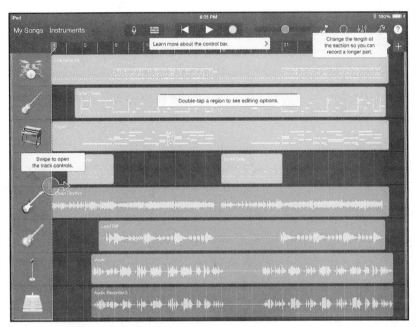

Figure 1.12 Sample GarageBand Help screen.

Press Play (the universal play triangle), as shown in Figure 1.13. Although the
iPad does a good job of playing through its speakers, you will want to plug in a
high-quality set of headphones or earbuds, or route the sound into a good set
of speakers for the best fidelity. For serious listeners (or composers/editors), a
comfortable listening arrangement will be invaluable.

Figure 1.13 Play button

You will notice that as you listen, the playhead moves across the screen, and the
music is marked with measures at the top of the screen, as shown in Figure 1.14.

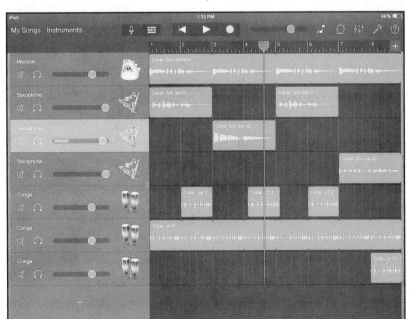

Figure 1.14 View of GarageBand screen when playing.

After you listen to the piece, tap My Songs in the top-left corner again (see Figure 1.15). We'll do more with this piece later, but for now, you should return to the song list.

The song list accomplishes many functions; as described earlier, one of the most significant is that it lists songs and allows you to select them for playback or further editing. The song list is also much like a computer's operating system. It allows you to copy, save, move, and delete files. Let's duplicate a song for our next activity so we can practice editing it. Most of the other file operations are accomplished in the same manner.

Duplicating a Song

To duplicate a song, first tap the Select button in the upper-right corner of the song list (see Figure 1.16). Next, tap the Celebration song, as shown in Figure 1.17, and then tap the Duplicate button (see Figure 1.18).

The iOS device will take a moment, but this sets us up for our next activity, which will be editing the demo song. Our edits could make things worse, so let's work from a copy instead of the original. When the file finishes duplicating, tap Done at the top of the screen (see Figure 1.19).

The name of the new file will be Celebration – copy. If you desire, you can rename the file by clicking its title once and then typing a new name.

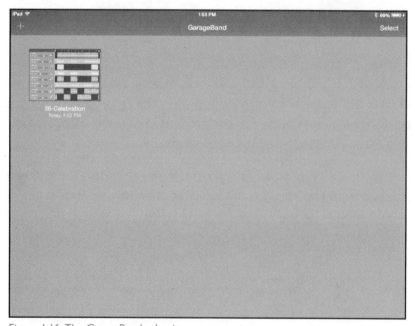

Figure 1.16 The GarageBand selection screen.

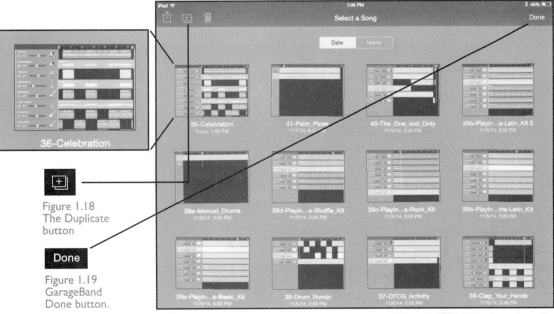

Figure 1.18
The Duplicate
button

Figure 1.19
GarageBand
Done button.

Figure 1.17 Celebration selected.

ACTIVITY 1: RECORDING A TRACK IN AN EXISTING GARAGEBAND SONG

To record a track in an existing GarageBand song, open the copy of the
GarageBand demo song by tapping its icon. At the bottom of the track should
be a + sign, as shown in Figure 1.20.

Figure 1.20 GarageBand
New Track button.

Tap the + sign. If the + sign is not visible, scroll past the last track (tap the track
data, and hold and drag the screen). The + sign will be visible at the bottom left
of the tracks, if not otherwise (see Figure 1.21).

Figure 1.21 GarageBand last track.

From the Instrument Selector screen that appears, there are many options for
tracks you can add to GarageBand. Each of these deserves consideration, but
for now, scroll left or right as needed and choose Audio Recorder, as shown in
Figure 1.22.

Figure 1.22 Select Audio Recorder.

Yet another GarageBand view will appear (see Figure 1.23). This is the **Audio Recording View**.

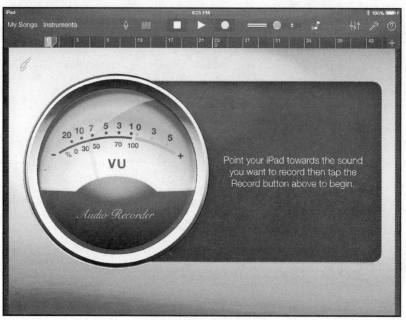

Figure 1.23 Audio Recorder instrument.

Figure 1.24 GarageBand Record button.

Figure 1.25 GarageBand Rewind button.

Figure 1.26 GarageBand Stop button.

Plug in headphones and ask everyone around you to remain quiet while you are recording. Next, tap Record at the top of the screen. The universal Record icon in virtually every production program is a red dot, as shown in Figure 1.24.

For your first vocal recording, add a vocal percussion line. If you are good at beat-box vocalizations, feel free to record anything you wish. If you feel uncomfortable with that process, simply record straight eighth notes on a syllable with all consonants, such as *tch* or *shp*, or some combination of them (*tch tch tch tch tch tch shp tch*).

If you make a mistake, repeat the process and record over the mistakes. (Tap Rewind, as shown in Figure 1.25, and then Record.)

You can record from any spot in the song by moving the playhead to the correct measure. Note: The default mode for recording most instruments is to replace the existing data in the track. Some instruments can be set to continually record additional layers to the same track. This is explained in more detail in the "Merge Recordings" section of Chapter 3.

When you finish recording, press the Stop button, shown in Figure 1.26.

You will be presented with a number of options for track effects. The default is no effect, but here is a quick list of the available options (see Figure 1.27). You can choose any of these you wish, but for now, none is recommended.

Figure 1.27 GarageBand effects selection for audio tracks.

- **Small Room.** This adds reverb (echoes) to the recording, as you might experience when performing in a small room. Reverb often enhances the original recording. The Compression slider and Original Signal slider select how much of each is applied to the track. See the glossary for an explanation of compression—or just experiment with different values.

- **Large Room.** This adds a reverb as might be experienced in a larger room.

- **Dreamy.** This adds reverb and additional chorus/echo.

- **Telephone.** This removes low and high frequencies, permitting only middle frequencies to pass, as would be common if recording audio from an analog telephone.

- **Dry.** This applies no effects.

- **Bullhorn.** This adds some amplification and clipping distortion.

- **Chipmunk.** This raises the pitch by an interval that is sure to not match the song. However, there is a pitch slider, which may permit you to put it in a useful range. Unless you can get this in tune, it is best to use this effect only on speech.

- **Robot.** This lowers the pitch by an interval that is sure to not match the song. Use it only on speech. There are adjustments for phaser and for chorus, but not for pitch. Experimenting with those values can yield some interesting results.

- **Monster.** This lowers the pitch by an octave. There is a pitch slider, which can be used for good effect on speech, but it is probably already set to the best value for music.

GarageBand will automatically use the built-in microphone of the iPad, iPhone, or other iOS device. Higher-quality external microphones are available at low cost if needed. Operating these external devices is simple. Typically, you plug an interface into the iPad, either in the headphone jack or the data port, and then plug a microphone or instrument into the interface. See the chapter on peripheral devices for more details.

To listen to your recording, press Rewind and then Play. You might need to balance the newly recorded track so you can hear it. If so, return to the track list (click the Track List icon, shown in Figure 1.28).

To see the volume control for each track, you may need to open the control area. To do so, touch the three light lines in the center of the screen (or the gray area below the last track) and swipe right to open (and left to close). See Figures 1.29 through 1.31.

Figure 1.28 GarageBand Track List icon.

Figure 1.29 Instructions for opening the control area.

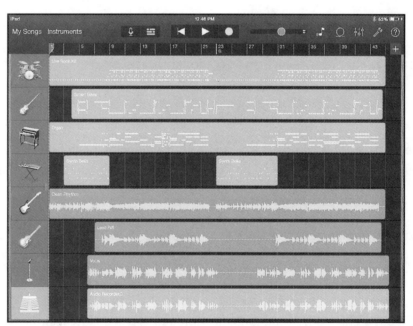

Figure 1.30 GarageBand Track view with controls hidden.

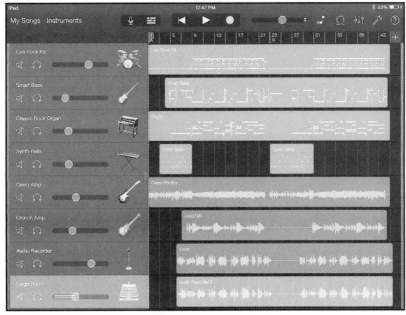

Figure 1.31 GarageBand Track view with controls open.

When the controls are open, you may see a volume slider for each track. If the recorded track is too soft, then drag its volume slider to the right, as shown in Figure 1.32.

If the recorded track is still too soft, you might need to turn down some of the other tracks (drag their sliders to the left). If the track is still too soft, you might need to record again with a louder source.

Two other useful buttons are available on the track controls: the Mute and Solo buttons. (See Figure 1.33.)

The speaker (or Mute button) turns off the corresponding track (see Figure 1.34).

The headphone (or Solo button) turns on only the track selected (see Figure 1.35).

You can use the Mute and Solo buttons in combination with one another. You can experiment with how your compositions might sound without a questionable track or with a simpler accompaniment. Use these buttons freely to experiment with compositions.

Figure 1.32 GarageBand track volume slider.

Figure 1.33 GarageBand track controls.

Figure 1.34 GarageBand Mute button.

Figure 1.35 GarageBand Solo button.

ACTIVITY 2: CREATING A NEW AUDIO TRACK AND REPLACING AN EXISTING AUDIO TRACK

Open the recording you created in Activity 1. Create a new audio track (press the + sign below the last track) and record yourself into this track singing the melody. You'll see the lyrics below. You can dowload a PDF of the music notation from *www.alfred.com/LearningGarageBand.* Be energetic and expressive. There is more to performing than just singing the right notes at the right time. Imitate the vocal expressions of the original performer. If you are inhibited as a singer or performer, you might want to request assistance from a performing friend. As before, when you're finished recording, you might need to adjust the level of the recorded track. Open the track controls and make adjustments as needed.

Celebration (Lyrics)

Chorus:
Celebrate, happy times.
Good times today, celebrate!
Celebrate, happy times,
Celebrate, celebrate, today!

Bridge:
There's a good time in the morning.
Sun is shining, celebration.

There's a good time in the evening.
In the moon light we'll celebrate.

Verse:
Every one, everywhere, everyday,
Let's celebrate, together we'll celebrate.
Everybody, let's celebrate,
We'll have a celebration, together we sing.

Celebration

Melody and Chords
Bess Harbison

Floyd Richmond

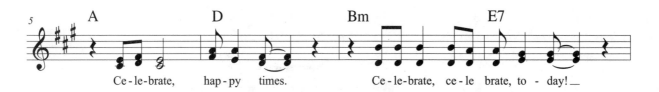

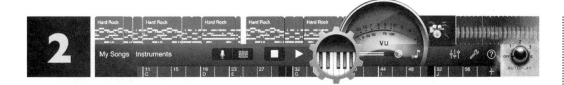

Chapter 2: Quickstart 2—Creating a Song Using Only Loops

One of GarageBand's great features is the large number of included prebuilt musical building blocks, called loops. You can compose songs using only these existing loops. For examples, check out Cuban Dance and Hip Hop Dance from Chapter 9 and the book's media site (*www.alfred.com/LearningGarageBand*).

ACTIVITY 1: USING LOOPS

For this activity, launch GarageBand, navigate to the song list, click the + button in the top-left corner of the screen (see Figure 2.1), and create a new GarageBand song.

GarageBand will immediately send you to the Instrument Selection list, shown in Figure 2.2.

Figure 2.1
GarageBand New
Song button.

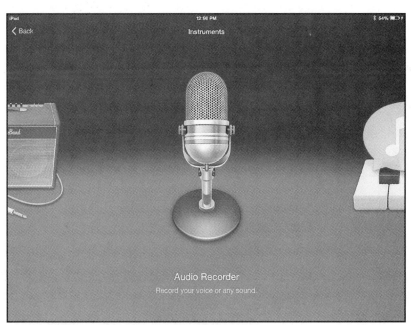

Figure 2.2 GarageBand Instrument Selection list.

To build a song with only loops, you must navigate to the Track View. This requires you to create an instrument track, even though you may not use it. For now, click Audio Recorder and then click the Track View button at the top of the screen, as shown in Figure 2.3.

Figure 2.3

GarageBand will create an empty track that you can delete later. To delete a track, tap its instrument icon and choose Delete from the menu that appears (see Figure 2.4).

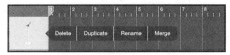

Figure 2.4 GarageBand Track Edit menu.

Figure 2.5
GarageBand
Loop button.

Figure 2.6 GarageBand Loop box.

To search for loops and listen to them, use the Loop Browser. Click the Loop button at the top of the screen, as shown in Figure 2.5.

The dialog box shown in Figure 2.6 will appear.

The current version of GarageBand can use three different types of audio, discusssed in the "Types of GarageBand Audio" sidebar and shown in Figure 2.7.

Figure 2.7 GarageBand loop types.

For this activity, we are using Apple Loops. Tap the Apple Loops tab at the top of the Loop Browser. Immediately below the Apple Loops tab is a search field. (See the "Searching for Apple Loops" sidebar on page 25.)

TYPES OF GARAGEBAND AUDIO

The current version of GarageBand has three types of audio that can be added to songs:

- **APPLE LOOPS**, which are the built-in musical building blocks of GarageBand. As of this writing, more than 250 loops are available in the iOS version of GarageBand.

- **AUDIO FILES**, which are audio files loaded into the GarageBand application using iTunes (see Figure 2.8). See Chapter 8 for information on exchanging files with GarageBand.

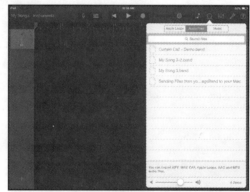

Figure 2.8 GarageBand Audio Files menu.

- **MUSIC FILES**, which are audio files from iTunes organized by album, artist, genre, playlist, and song.

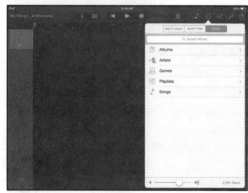

Figure 2.9 GarageBand Music menu.

SEARCHING FOR APPLE LOOPS

By typing keywords into the loops search field, as shown in Figure 2.10, you can find music for different instruments in the same style.

Figure 2.10 GarageBand loop search by keywords.

GarageBand's Loop Browser also has a number of additional search features. For example, you can search loops by the instrument used. If you select instruments, the following options will appear in a submenu: All Drums, Kits, Bass, Guitars, Side Guitar, Synths, Strings, Electric Piano, Mallets, Percussion, Shaker, Conga, Tambourine, Bongo, Woodwind, and Vocals. See Figure 2.11.

You can also search a number of musical genres or styles as follows: Country, Electronic, Experimental, Jazz, Orchestral, Other Genre, Rock/Blues, Urban, World. See Figure 2.12.

Figure 2.11 GarageBand loop search by instrument.

Finally, you can search by a number of contrasting musical descriptors, as follows: Single, Ensemble, Clean, Distorted, Acoustic, Electric, Relaxed, Intense, Cheerful, Dark, Dry, Processed, Grooving Arrhythmic, Melodic, Dissonant, Part, Fill. See Figure 2.13.

Some loops are grayed and cannot be selected. They are included for future expansion.

Figure 2.12 GarageBand loop search by genre.

By using these filters in your search, you can often find compatible materials to use for compositions built using loops and to supplement existing songs.

The results of searches are cumulative. That is, you can search, for example, for drum kits that are Electronic or that are Intense. If you'd like to clear previous searches, tap Reset Keywords in the Loop Browser, as shown in Figure 2.14.

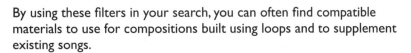

Figure 2.13 GarageBand loop search by description.

Reset Keywords

Figure 2.14 GarageBand loop search Reset button.

Because GarageBand includes more than 250 loops, it can find loops in a number of complementary and contrasting styles. Some of the loops work well together, and some do not. It is generally a good idea to use loops of the same style together. For example, a folk guitar would not necessarily sound good in a dance piece—although sometimes unusual combinations do work. A wonderful feature of GarageBand is that it enables just that kind of experimentation.

In the search field under Apple Loops, type the word Cuba, as shown in Figure 2.15.

Figure 2.15 GarageBand loop search for Cuba.

As of this writing, GarageBand will return seven loops. You may have to scroll up or down to see them all. Six are shown in Figure 2.16.

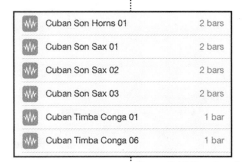

Figure 2.16 Results of GarageBand loop search for Cuba.

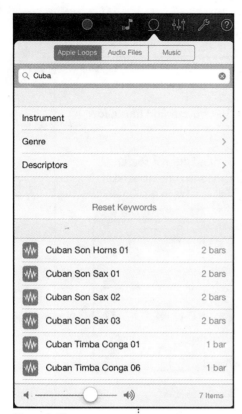

Figure 2.17
GarageBand loop
audition options.

You can listen to any loop by tapping it. There is a volume slider at the bottom of the screen that lets you adjust the volume as desired.

Listen to each loop by tapping on it. Tapping the original loop again will stop the playback. Tapping another loop will stop playback of the first loop and begin playback of the next.

This search (Cuba) is a great first activity because each of these seven loops can be played together without any harmonic clashes. While the style of each of these loops is similar, it is important to use those that are melodic and those that are rhythmic appropriately. The melodic loops, which would best be used one at a time, are sax, horns, and so on. The rhythmic loops, which can be used simultaneously with any other loops, are congas.

To use a loop in a song, drag it from the Loop Browser to the timeline of the song.

Note that there are two different types of loops used in GarageBand: digital audio and MIDI. The two are distinguished in GarageBand by their color—digital audio loops are blue, and MIDI loops are green—and by the images used on the various tracks to represent the data that they contain (see Figure 2.18). Digital audio tracks look like they contain audio waves, which represent recordings of actual instruments. MIDI tracks look like bubbles, and each bubble represents a note in the track to be played on an electronic instrument. For our purposes at this time, these differences aren't too important. Both digital audio and MIDI loops may be used in the same manner. Differences will be more apparent when you're editing them.

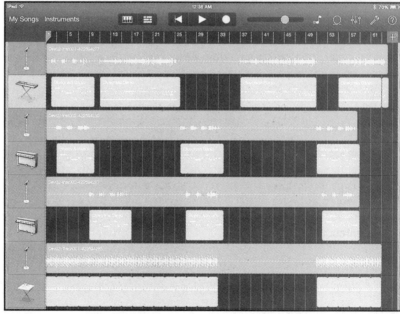

Figure 2.18 GarageBand MIDI and digital audio data.

To complete this activity, drag the loops to different tracks in the GarageBand window, and edit and position them as desired. (See the "Editing Loops" sidebar on page 27.)

Figure 2.19 shows a good combination of the Cuban loops in an eight-bar song. Re-create this song to master working with loops. If you finish before your classmates, create a version of your own design. (To create a second song, tap My Songs and then tap the + button to create a second version.)

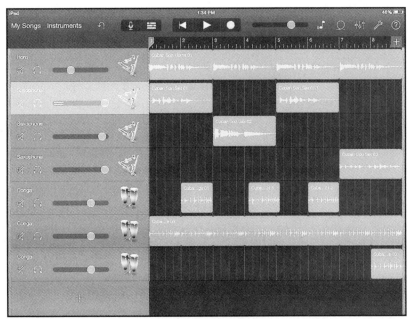

Figure 2.19 GarageBand Cuban Loops song example.

EDITING LOOPS

GarageBand will automatically repeat the loop from the point you dropped it into the song to the end of the section. If you want a loop to play only one time, tap it and then drag the loop icon at the end until the loop is the desired length. If you want this loop to play at a different time, you can drag it to the left or right until it aligns with the desired measure. (See the ruler at the top of the screen that shows measure numbers, shown in Figure 2.20.)

Figure 2.20 GarageBand ruler showing measures.

If you want a loop to play multiple times with rests between, the easiest way to accomplish this is to drag it from the Apple Loops into the same track again, shortening and positioning it as desired. Alternatively, you may copy and paste an existing loop in a track. To copy and paste a loop, tap it, select Copy from the menu that appears, move the playhead to the desired location in the track, tap in the track (to make certain nothing else is selected), and choose Paste from the menu that appears. If you paste a loop at the end of a track, into a space in which it won't fit, only the portion that will fit will be pasted.

If you wish to undo a copy/paste or move operation, tap the Undo button at the top of the screen (see Figure 2.21).

You can tap Undo multiple times to undo several operations. The Undo function is invaluable, so it's good to be thoroughly acquainted with it. The Undo button even has a special feature so that if you inadvertently undo something, you can tap and hold it, and a menu will appear permitting you to redo an operation (see Figure 2.22).

Figure 2.21 GarageBand Undo button.

Practice with the Undo button until you have mastered it.

One last note about loops: sometimes, loops don't sound correct together when played at the same volume, but they do if one is made softer. To view a track's volume control, tap the gray area beneath the last track and slide right. There are also lines on the right middle of the tracks that can be used to slide open the track's volume controls. Adjust each track's volume as desired.

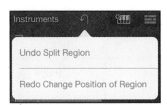

Figure 2.22 GarageBand Undo/Redo menu.

A Few Additional Notes

GarageBand for iOS has some features that are unique among music production programs. Two areas that may seem unusual to those just beginning to use GarageBand or to those experienced with other music production programs are its approach to the length of a song and the approach to editing sections. Also, for those who may be new to working with musical loops, tips are found below.

Song Length

For this activity, GarageBand defaults to eight-measure songs (or song sections). You can adjust this using the + sign at the top right of the screen (see Figure 2.23).

Tapping the + sign reveals the menu shown in Figure 2.24.

Click the default length of 8 bars, and the screen shown in Figure 2.25 will appear.

You can manually adjust the length of the song to any number of measures. Figure 2.26 shows 24.

During recording, GarageBand will automatically loop back to the beginning after reaching the number of measures specified.

Alternatively, you can switch to automatic mode, where GarageBand will not impose a limit on how long the song is but will keep recording until you tap the Stop button. See Figures 2.27 and 2.28.

Figure 2.23 GarageBand song section and length editor (+ sign).

Figure 2.24 GarageBand Song Sections menu.

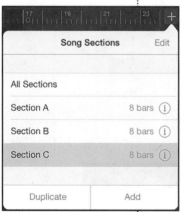

Figure 2.25 GarageBand Section Length menu.

Figure 2.26 GarageBand Section Length selector: 24 measures.

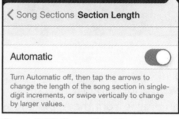

Figure 2.27 GarageBand Section Length selector: Automatic.

Figure 2.28 GarageBand Stop button.

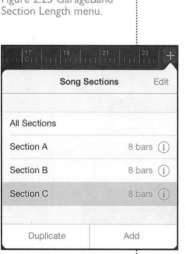

Figure 2.29 GarageBand Section Length editor: three sections.

It is a good idea to think about which strategy would be more useful. Often, people find it easier to record in eight- or sixteen-measure blocks (roughly corresponding to the length of a verse or chorus of a pop song). If you record in eight-measure blocks, you may want to use the Duplicate and Add buttons shown at the bottom of Figure 2.24.

The Duplicate button makes a copy of a selected section and adds it to the list. (If the first section were Section A, the duplicated section would be Section B.) The Add button creates a new empty section. Each new duplicated or added section can be set to a specific number of measures or set to automatic length.

Editing Sections

Tapping the Edit button in the Section Editor box provides additional options. If you want to reorder the sections, you can simply drag them to the desired order. For example, you could move Section A after Section C.

If you would like to delete a section, tap the minus sign (-) and then Delete (see Figures 2.30 and 2.31).

If you composed your song in multiple sections, you need to select All Sections in order to play or work with the whole song.

Figure 2.30 GarageBand Section Length selector: delete selection.

Working with GarageBand Loops

This section will give you several tips for working with GarageBand loops. An important consideration when working with GarageBand loops is harmony. GarageBand loops usually use one or two chords each. When combining loops, it is important to do so in a manner that does not create harmonic dissonance. That is, unless the loops use the same harmonic progression (chords), they should be played one after the other, rather than at the same time.

The bad news is, it is not always possible to determine in advance which loops are harmonically compatible and can be used together. The good news is, GarageBand often uses loops with only one chord that will work with any other loops with the same chords. And furthermore, if you listen, your ears will quickly tell you whether there is a harmonic problem. The general rule of thumb is that if a combination of loops sounds good to a large number of people, then it is good. If a combination sounds good to just one or a few people, then those loops should not be used together.

Figure 2.31 GarageBand Section Length selector: delete selection confirmation.

As long as they are playing complementary rhythms, percussion instruments go together regardless of harmony. It is a good idea to begin by putting the percussion tracks into the song, then adding melodic and harmonic instruments until you reach the desired textures.

ACTIVITY 2: COMBINING LOOPS AND RECORDING

Open the song you created in Activity 1. Add an additional track by clicking the + sign at the bottom of the track list. Record a vocal track. Be creative, but here is a suggestion: At the end of every phrase (every two measures), exclaim one of the following utterances (or another of your own):

That's right!
Play it!
You got it!
Sing it!
Keep it going!
Uh huh!
That's it!
Yep!

Now that you've recorded an original song (using Apple Loops), it's time to share the results with the world. Tap My Songs, tap Select, tap your song (a blue

Figure 2.32 GarageBand Share button.

Figure 2.33 GarageBand share options.

frame will appear around it), and then tap the Share button (a box with an arrow pointing upward; see Figure 2.32).

Apps for iOS tend to permit immediate sharing of their products with cloud-based computing services, and GarageBand is no exception. Among GarageBand's options for cloud-based sharing are Mail, Facebook, SoundCloud, and YouTube, as shown in Figure 2.33.

Selecting Mail causes GarageBand to compress and attach an MP4 audio file to an email message. You can then send a copy to yourself or others. Note: You must have properly configured the mail application with email credentials for this to work. If you have not done this yet, you can do so in iOS Settings > Mail, Contacts, and Calendars. You must create an account with a link to your email server, a username, and a password. You must also have a connection to the Internet from your iOS device. This connection may be wireless or cellular.

Selecting Facebook causes GarageBand to compress an MP4 file and post it to your timeline. You may be asked to sign in to Facebook, if your Facebook account information has not been entered into the iOS settings. Like before, you must have a wireless or cellular connection to the Internet for GarageBand to share your file.

Selecting SoundCloud posts an MP4 to that service. One great advantage of SoundCloud is that listeners can post comments tied to individual moments in the music. This is especially helpful for teachers who may want to make suggestions for improvements to specific sections of the music.

Selecting YouTube posts an MP4 to that service in one of three levels of privacy: private, unlisted, or public.

- **Private.** When a video is private, it can be shared only with another Gmail user. While private may sound like a good choice to the timid student, private files are more difficult to share with the teacher than other files.

- **Unlisted.** When a video is unlisted, it may be shared with anyone—but only if the person wishing to view it has the video's URL. The only source of that URL is the person posting the video. Unlisted YouTube videos are not indexed in the YouTube database of videos, and it is unlikely that anyone other than someone to whom the URL has been sent will see the video.

- **Public.** If a video is posted as public, then it is available to anyone on the Internet. The most likely way that someone will see it will be if the creator has shared the URL; however, YouTube also enters the video into its database, and it is possible for other people to find the video by searching for its title or keywords associated with it.

Chapter 3: Quickstart 3—Playing and Recording GarageBand's Instruments

GarageBand has an excellent collection of virtual instruments you can play manually and automatically. With appropriate amplification, you can use these instruments as part of a live ensemble, or you can record and edit them within GarageBand. The instruments available as of this writing are:

Keyboard: manually controlled piano, organ, and synthesizer.

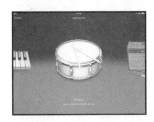

Drums: manually controlled drumset.

Sampler: manually controlled keyboard with included and user-defined sampled sound effects.

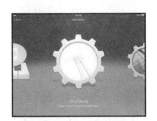

Smart Drums: a drum machine that allows users to select the style of drums (hip-hop, classic, and house drum machines and classic, vintage, and live-rock drum kits) and to program the drums to play simple or complex patterns with loud or soft combinations of instruments.

Smart Strings: a string sampler with four styles of strings (cinematic, modern, pop, and romantic). It can play various combinations of string instruments on user-controlled chords using up to four automatic patterns for each style. Users may also switch to note mode and play individual notes on any stringed instrument in pizzicato or bowed style.

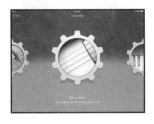

Smart Bass: a bass sampler with eight styles of bass (Liverpool, muted, picked, upright, exoplanet, light cycle, retro bass, and sequence bass). It can play user-controlled chords using up to four automatic patterns for each style. Users may also switch to note mode and play individual notes.

Smart Keyboard: a keyboard sampler with eight styles of piano (grand piano, classic rock organ, electric piano, smooth clavier, helix, machine language, polarize, and solar sailor). It can play user-controlled chords using up to four automatic patterns for each style. Users may also play individual notes from specified chords or roll chords. The instrument also has an arpeggiator that can be programmed to produce various patterns.

Smart Guitar: a guitar sampler with four styles of guitar (acoustic, classic clean, hard rock, and roots rock). It can play user-controlled chords using up to four automatic patterns for each style. Users may also play individual notes or strum chords.

Additionally, GarageBand has several other "instruments" that are more for the purpose of recording.

Guitar Amp: a digital audio recording track that is set up for guitars (with classic amps and effects pedals). This option requires an adapter to receive input from an electric guitar. (See Chapter 10 on external devices and peripherals.) It is possible to use this "instrument" as an effects box for live performance on an attached guitar, but its greatest use will be for recording.

Audio Recorder: a digital audio recording track that uses the built-in microphone or other available microphones to record vocals or instruments.

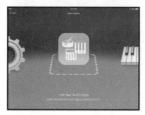

Inter-App Audio Apps: a mechanism for recording from other apps that use the same sound architecture. This is available only if you have compatible applications (and Audio Bus is not running on your iPad). Choose this option and select the app from which you would like to record. Tap on its icon and press Record from within that app. Play along with the GarageBand metronome. When you're finished, tap the GarageBand icon in that app to return to GarageBand.

ACTIVITY 1: RECORDING DRUMS MANUALLY

Launch GarageBand, and from the song list, create a new song (click +, as shown in Figure 3.1).

Figure 3.1 GarageBand New Song button.

GarageBand will automatically launch the Instrument Selection view, shown in Figure 3.2. (If you are adding a track to an existing song, then navigate to the Track View window and then click the + button at the bottom of the tracks.)

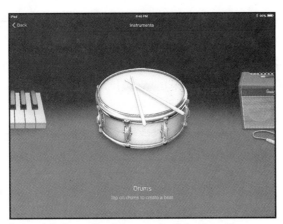

Figure 3.2 GarageBand Instrument Selection view: Drums.

Select Drums, and the screen shown in Figure 3.3 will appear.

Figure 3.3 GarageBand Classic Studio Kit.

Choose the desired drum machine from the various possibilities (hip-hop, classic, and house drum machines; and classic, vintage, and live-rock drum kits, as shown in Figure 3.4).

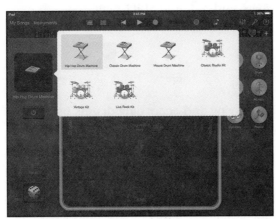

Figure 3.4 GarageBand drum kit options.

Figure 3.1 GarageBand New Song button.

Each drum kit has unique sounds. Regardless of which kit you choose, before recording, it's a good idea to practice your part.

To create a simple drumbeat follow these steps. Count to 4 a total of 8 times (8 measures), play the bass drum on 1 and 3 of every measure and the snare drum on 2 and 4 of every measure. Record cymbals on eighth notes (open and closed hi-hats and crash cymbal) and toms on Beats 3 and 4 of Measures 4 and 8 only.

When you're ready to perform, tap Record, as shown in Figure 3.5.

Because it is difficult to record all the drums in one pass, the default mode when recording from this instrument is to keep recording for as many passes as desired. This option, called *Merge Recordings*, can be toggled on and off in the track menu, if desired (see Figure 3.6).

If this option is off, recording is done only on the first pass. Merge Recordings is only available on manually played instruments (keyboard and drums) and not on smart instruments.

The best strategy would be to record snare and bass in the first pass. On a second pass, record cymbals on eighth notes (open and closed hi-hats and crash cymbal). On a third pass, add toms on Beats 3 and 4 of Measures 4 and 8 only.

Listen to your creation. If you aren't pleased, tap Undo and Rewind, as shown in Figures 3.7 and 3.8, and start over.

Figure 3.5 GarageBand Record button.

Figure 3.6 GarageBand Merge Recordings option.

Figure 3.7 Undo button.

Figure 3.8 Rewind button.

Additional tips on playing and recording drums using a MIDI keyboard or drum controller are found in Chapter 10.

MERGE RECORDINGS

Because Merge Recordings is turned on by default with manually recorded instruments (keyboards and drums), you must undo (or erase the previous recording) before recording again. Alternatively, you can replace a previous recording by recording over it a second time by turning off Merge Recordings in the track menu.

For smart instruments, Merge Recordings is not available, so you can replace them by recording over them at any time.

NOTE: Merge Recordings is a setting which permits instruments to be recorded on top of each other in the same track during the recording process. GarageBand also supports a Merge Track feature which combines multiple tracks. Merge Tracks is useful when the maximum number of tracks is exceeded. To Merge Tracks, tap the instrument icon of a track, and select Merge Tracks from the menu which appears. Select which tracks should be merged, then tap Merge at the top right of the screen. GarageBand will automatically duplicate the song before merging tracks. The copy of the song will then contain the only remaining record of the unmerged tracks.

ACTIVITY 2: RECORDING DRUMS AUTOMATICALLY

Launch GarageBand, and from the song list create a new song (click +). GarageBand will automatically launch the Instrument Selection view. (If you are adding a track to an existing song, then navigate to the Track View window and then click the + button at the bottom of the tracks.) Select Smart Drums, as shown in Figure 3.9.

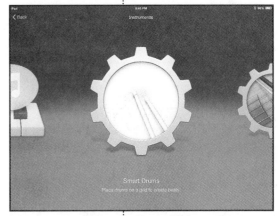

Figure 3.9 Instrument Selection view: Smart Drums.

The screen shown in Figure 3.10 will appear.

Next, choose the desired drum machine from the various possibilities. The same drum machines as for the manual drums are available. Tap the Die button to have the computer randomly select some instruments and position them on the screen. Listen to the computer's drum kit. If you like it, skip ahead. If not, then tap the Die button to have GarageBand suggest another rhythm. Alternatively, you can adjust the rhythmic accompaniment as follows.

1. Drag any instrument playing softly higher and any instrument playing too loudly lower.

2. Drag any instrument playing too simple a part to the right and any instrument playing too busily to the left.

3. Drag any instruments you'd like to remove from the accompaniment off the screen.

4. Drag any instruments you'd like to add to the accompaniment to the screen and position them as desired for volume (high = loud, low = soft) and for rhythmic activity (left = simple, right = complex).

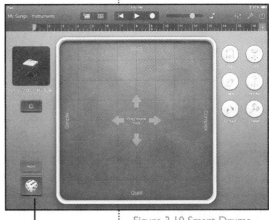

DIE BUTTON

Figure 3.10 Smart Drums Performance and Settings view.

The drum machine creates all parts in one pass and does not provide a Merge Recording option. Record the drums and listen to the result. If you aren't pleased, tap Undo and start over.

For a basic drum accompanying pattern, put the snare and bass near the top of Column 1. Put the hi-hat near the top middle of the screen. Put the ride cymbal near the top right of the screen. The pattern that is generated (except for the ride cymbal) is used more often than any other and is similar to the first pattern any beginning student learning the drumset would play. Move instruments to the right to make their patterns more complex.

NOTE: GarageBand SmartDrums currently do not swing. If you need drums that swing, choose drum loops, and select the shuffle drummer.

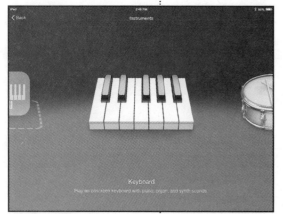

Figure 3.11 Instrument Selection view: Keyboard.

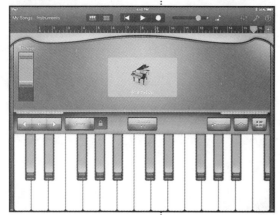

Figure 3.12 Keyboard Performance and Settings view.

ACTIVITY 3: RECORDING KEYBOARD MANUALLY

Launch GarageBand, and from the song list create a new song (click +). GarageBand will automatically launch the Instrument Selection view. (If you are adding a track to an existing song, then navigate to the Track View window and then click the + button at the bottom of the tracks.) Select Keyboard, as shown in Figure 3.11.

The screen shown in Figure 3.12 will appear.

Next, choose the desired keyboard from the various possibilities, as shown in Figure 3.13.

Tap Record. Play the melody you wish to record on the keyboard. (See a suggested melody on page 37.) When you're finished, listen to your creation. If you aren't pleased, tap Undo and start over.

If you want to play the melody an octave higher or lower, press the left or right arrow button above the left side of the keyboard. The button between the two arrows shows the octave in which the notes will sound, and when tapped, it returns the keyboard to its original setting.

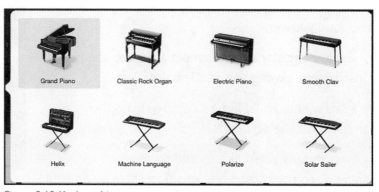

Figure 3.13 Keyboard instrument options.

ACTIVITY 4: RECORDING KEYBOARDS AUTOMATICALLY

Open the song you recorded in Activity 3. (You may want to duplicate it first, because we will be changing it in this activity.) Create a new track (click +). GarageBand will automatically launch the Instrument Selection view. Select Smart Keyboard, as shown in Figure 3.14.

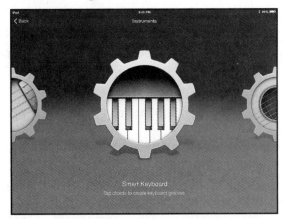

Figure 3.14 Instrument Selection view: Smart Keyboard.

The screen shown in Figure 3.15 will appear.

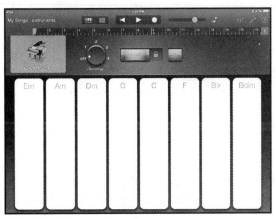

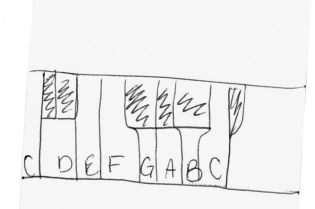

Figure 3.15 Smart Keyboard.

Next, choose the desired keyboard from the various possibilities. Th options are available as on the manual piano: Grand Piano, Classic R Electric Piano, Smooth Clavier, Helix, Machine Language, Polarize, and Solar Sailor.

If you aren't certain which instrument to use, a good first choice would be grand piano; however, you should experiment with these so you are aware of the sounds of the other instruments.

Tap Record and then play the chords for the previously recorded song. (Notice the chords on the music on page 37.)

When recording these, it's okay to use creative rhythms on the chords. However, if you're uncertain, then simply playing whole-note chords is a good way to begin.

There are several ways to play chords using GarageBand's Smart Keyboard. You can use the different methods one after the other, but only one at a time. Undo or delete the previous recording and experiment with each of these. If you are particularly pleased with one result, you may want to save it and open a copy of Activity 3 to create another accompaniment.

1. **Tap the chord bar on the desired chord:** Tap low on the bar for a low chord and high for a high chord (or anywhere in between). The bottom three buttons play a single bass note from the chord, and the upper area (white) plays chords in various ranges. Hold the button down to sustain the chord, and tap and release for staccato. You can "roll" the chord by moving your finger slowly across the bar from low to high.

2. **Auto-accompaniment:** GarageBand has four selectable piano accompaniments for each instrument. Choose one and experiment with the instrument to see what sounds it will play. Tap the chord name for the easiest accompaniment. If you like to experiment with some more adventurous chords—for example, C/G (a C chord over the note G)—you can tap the bottom part of the chord bar under the G chord and the middle part under the C chord. Using this technique, you can play most chords commonly used in popular music.

3. **Arpeggiator:** To turn on the arpeggiator, tap the Arpeggiator button and slide the Run switch to on (see Figure 3.16). When the arpeggiator options appear, as shown in Figure 3.17, set those. The defaults are fine, but experiment with different values, especially with slower-valued notes (1/8 notes, for example) and with a narrower or wider range (one octave, and so on). Finally, play the arpeggiator using the same chord bar as in #1 above with the same options for low and high chords.

The Smart Keyboard creates all parts in one pass and does not provide a Merge Recording option, so record everything in one pass. Listen to the result. If you aren't pleased, tap Undo, rewind, and start over.

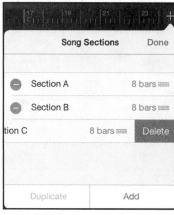

Figure 3.16 Arpeggiator on/off switch.

Figure 3.17 Arpeggiator options.

ACTIVITY 5: RECORDING WITH OTHER SMART INSTRUMENTS

Repeat Activity 4 with Smart Strings, Smart Guitar, and Smart Bass (adding extra tracks to Activity 3). Duplicate Activity 3 before you begin. If you add additional layers to the piano accompaniment above, the texture may be too thick.

The process for recording with other smart instruments is basically the same as for the keyboard, especially in any of the chord modes.

1. Select the instrument sound.

2. Tap Record.

3. Play the chords.

One difference is that the strings, guitar, and bass do not have an arpeggiator mode. Another difference is that all string instruments have a note mode for playing melodies, which is not available in Smart Keyboards (although it is available in the regular Keyboard instrument).

Here are some other important differences:

- Guitars may strum the chord bar in either direction, whereas it is more common for pianists to play from low to high.

- The strings may be bowed by moving your finger across the chord bar or played pizzicato by tapping the chord bar.

- The bass normally plays only one note at a time as a performance tradition. Strumming all bass strings at once is not recommended. When you strike bass chords in GarageBand, you will only hear one note.

For now, record a track for strings, a track for guitar, and a track for bass using the chords that you performed earlier. Feel free to experiment with the rhythms, but don't be "too busy" rhythmically.

Now that you've expanded your composition to include the other instruments, record the melody on a melodic instrument. You may want to create a new song for these experiments.

On each smart instrument, look for a switch that says Notes. The appearance of the screen will change, so that instead of seeing a chord bar that you can strum or bow, you will see individual strings and frets (on the guitar and bass guitar), and position markers on the strings. Because the instruments look very much like an actual instrument, it's beneficial to have played these instruments before. If you have not played them, your ears will help you find the right notes.

Let's wrap up with a few tips.

You need these four notes for "Mary Had a Little Lamb": C, D, E, and G. The position of each of these is given below.

Guitar

C = 2nd string (B string), 1st fret
D = 2nd string, 3rd fret
E = 1st string (E string), open
G = 1st string, 3rd fret

Bass

C = 3rd string (A string), 3rd fret
D = 2nd string (D string), open
E = 2nd string, 2nd fret
G = 1st string (G string), open

Violin

C = 2nd string (A string), 1st dot
D = 2nd string, 2nd dot
E = 1st string (E string), open
G = 1st string, 3rd dot

Viola, Cello

C = 4th string (C string), open
D = 4th string, low on 1st dot
E = 4th string, between dots 2 and 3
G = 3rd string (G string), open

String Bass

C = 3rd string (A string), 1st dot
D = 2nd string (D string), open
E = 2nd string, low on 1st dot
G = 1st string (G string), open

There is one significant difference between playing melodies on GarageBand instruments and on actual instruments, and it is that open strings require a finger to touch the string at the top of the neck. This means that virtual instruments are, in this regard, harder to play than their actual counterparts. Because you don't have to use both hands to play the virtual instruments, however, this problem is usually easily solved.

There is one special circumstance for playing notes on strings (violin, viola, cello, and bass) that needs attention. By default, these instruments play bowed notes. If you'd like to play pizzicato (plucked), you must press the bronze-colored pizzicato icon at the top of the fingerboard while tapping the notes (see Figure 3.18).

At this point, you should have a good command of how to use GarageBand for iOS. The following chapters will take you deeper into your understanding of creating recordings of existing and original music in GarageBand. You'll also find additional music to record and perform.

Congratulations on having completed the Quickstart section of the book!

Figure 3.18 GarageBand pizzicato and bowing selector.

Chapter 4: Using the GarageBand Sampler

One of the unique instruments in GarageBand is its sampler. This keyboard-controlled instrument lets you select or record a custom sound and then play melodies or chords with that sound. Does GarageBand for Mac have an English horn sound? Perhaps not, but if you record a note played by an actual English horn, GarageBand can then play an entire scale using that sound.

Using the Sampler

GarageBand's sampler has an increasing set of features that make it worthwhile, but it also has some limitations. In general terms, GarageBand permits the recording of new samples, the use of a library of existing samples, and the importing of audio files that can be used as samples. Its primary limitation is that at this point, it scales all notes it uses from a single sample. While this works well for pure, clear sounds, it doesn't work as well for complex waveforms. Most professional-level samplers use different recordings for each note. Until GarageBand for iOS can implement this strategy, it produces the best effects with the following types of pure sounds:

- Bell-like sounds

- Flute-like sounds

- Clarinet-like sounds

- Simple waveforms, such as triangle waves and sawtooth waves

That is not to say you shouldn't use more complex sounds. Often a sampled instrument works well in an ensemble, even if it might sound somewhat unusual when played alone. Furthermore, it is sometimes suprising how well some acoustic instruments work with GarageBand. Complex sounds may also sometimes be used to produce a comedic effect—for example, a normal recording of a voice (sample) can be transformed to sound high, like a chipmunk, or low, like a monster. These effects can often be used effectively in music.

Figure 4.1 Instrument Selection view: Sampler.

Figure 4.2 Sampler Performance and Settings view.

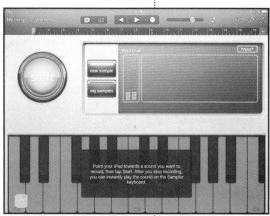

Figure 4.3 Creating a new sample.

Playing an Existing Sample

To play an existing sample, create a new GarageBand song, add an instrument, and choose the keyboard sampler (see Figure 4.1).

From the screen that appears, click on My Samples and select an existing sound. Some years ago, a version of "Jingle Bells" that featured a series of dog barks at various pitches became popular. Select the dog barking sample and create your own version (see Figure 4.2). To see the potential of the sampler, select each of the sounds and play a scale.

Recording a New Sample

To record a sound on the sampler, tap the New Sample button, tap Start, and then sing or play a single note (see Figure 4.3). Tap Stop and then play a scale or song using your sampled note.

GarageBand's sampler has some nice features for shaping the note. After the note is recorded, the sound could be played exactly as recorded, but sound engineers have found that many additional expressive possibilities are available if the shape (or envelope) is changed as each recorded note is played. With GarageBand, you can edit the sound's *envelope* as follows:

- *Attack* (how quickly the note rises to full volume)

- *Decay* (how quickly the note falls from the peak attack level to the sustain level)

- *Sustain* (how long the note is sustained)

- *Release* (how quickly the note decays after the note is released)

This attack, decay, sustain, release (ADSR) envelope is a common control feature on many electronic instruments, and you can find it on other GarageBand instruments, although it is not always as easily edited as in the sampler.

Notice the Import button on the screen in Figure 4.3. You can select any sound from your iTunes Library or your iTunes file-sharing files to use as a sample. The book comes with a number of sounds that may be used with the sampler. These samples are for instruments that are often needed in orchestrations, but that are not normally found in, GarageBand. To find these sounds, navigate to the books website: *www.alfred.com/ LearningGarageBand*

At the top of the next page is the list of sounds that are included in the Samples Folder of the downloadble materials for this book.

c-acousticguitar.wav	c-timpaniroll.wav
c-banjo.wav	c-trumpet.wav
c-bassoon.wav	c-tuba.wav
c-cello.wav	c-violin.wav
c-chimes.wav	c-xylophone.wav
c-clarinet.wav	perc-Agogo-High1.wav
c-flute.wav	perc-Agogo-Low1.wav
c-glockenspiel.wav	perc-Djembe1.wav
c-harp.wav	perc-Djembe2.wav
c-marimba.wav	perc-Djembe3.wav
c-oboe.wav	perc-Djembe4.wav
c-palmpipes.wav	perc-Djun-High.wav
c-saxophone.wav	perc-Djun-Low.wav
c-timpani.wav	perc-Djun-Med.wav

A sound that comes with this book and makes a great instrument is c-palmpipe.wav. Import that sound and play a scale.

IMPORTING A SOUND INTO GARAGEBAND'S SAMPLER

On a laptop or desktop computer, navigate to the book's media files.

Right-click any sound from the list above and save it where it can be found—for example, on the desktop or document folder.

Place the songs in your iTunes Library and sync them to the iPad.

With the iPad connected to the computer, click the "Import" button in the sampler and search for the file.

Note that the palm-pipe sound works well over many different octaves. It is the sound of the palm of a hand striking an open pipe. If you have seen or heard the Blue Man Group play on television or in person, you have heard similar sounds. Boomwhackers™ also make a similar sound.

ACTIVITIES

Activity: Listen to a Blue Man Group song from YouTube. Compose a song that sounds like that performance, using the c-palmpipe.wav sound.

Activity: Navigate to Chapter 9 and load song 41. Listen to the composition that uses the Palm Pipes sound.

Chapter 5: Other GarageBand Operations

When you're composing a song, you need to set or check a number of options early in the process. The most important ones are the key signature, time signature, and tempo. Also, you often need to be able to turn the metronome on and off. The options to do all these tasks are found in the Settings menu. Tap the wrench tool at the top of the GarageBand toolbar to access the menu.

The Settings Menu

To turn the metronome on and off, move the slider to the left for off and to the right for on (see Figure 5.1).

The count-in is a measure of clicks that will sound before recording. The Count-In option is turned on and off in the same manner as the Metronome option.

The sound (Woodblock in Figure 5.1) is the sound that will be used for the metronome and count-in. By selecting the Sound submenu (see Figure 5.2), you can select other metronome sounds.

You can also select the Tempo, Key, and Time Signature options from the Settings menu. If you are uncertain about any of these options, they default to excellent values, but for slower or faster songs or for songs in different keys, the Settings menu will be useful. Each option produces its own submenu (see Figures 5.3 through 5.5).

Figure 5.1 GarageBand Settings menu.

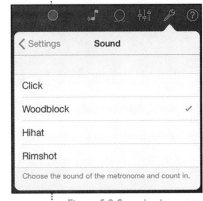

Figure 5.2 Sound submenu.

Figure 5.3 Key submenu.

Figure 5.4 Time Signature submenu.

Figure 5.5 Tempo submenu.

The Fade-Out menu option will be explained in the "Automatic Fade-Outs" section later in this chapter.

Run in Background is an on-off setting that permits GarageBand songs to be played while other programs are running. This is useful if, for example, you are using GarageBand songs to accompany other programs (such as slideshows or Keynote presentations, although there are other ways to add background music to those apps).

Airplay – Bluetooth is an on-off setting that allows the GarageBand audio output to be directed to wireless airplay speakers that may be in the area. Airplay technology has been around for a while and is supported by various speakers, Apple Express routers, and Apple TV. If you don't have these options available, then you will be using the iPad's speakers, headphones, or earbuds to listen. Airplay speakers are convenient because they permit wireless connections to external speakers.

Copy and Paste

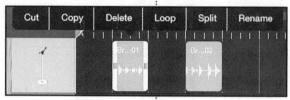

Figure 5.6 Edit menu.

If you're familiar with word processing software, you're undoubtedly acquainted with the process of copying material from one section and pasting it into another. GarageBand permits the same operations for music on several levels. In Figure 5.6, the blocks representing digital audio have been double-tapped, and the Edit menu, permitting the selected block or blocks to be copied, has appeared.

Tap Copy, and the computer's short-term memory will be loaded with a copy of the selected material. To paste, move the playhead to the desired point and double-tap again. A Paste option will appear; choose it, and a copy of that material will be placed at the playhead.

It is also possible to copy and paste blocks of MIDI data (the green blocks), as well as individual MIDI notes, when in MIDI Edit view.

The other options in the Edit menu (Cut, Copy, Delete, Loop, Split, and Rename) are generally self-explanatory. The only tool that may require a bit of explanation is the Split tool. To use it, move the playhead to the location where the split is desired, double-tap the block, and choose Split. Scissors will appear for you to move down across the track at the playhead. Afterward, you can select and copy or paste the block of musical material on either side of the cut.

Cut makes a copy of the selected material in the computer's short-term memory and removes that material from the score; copy does the same while leaving the original material in place.

Edit Track Properties

Earlier in Quickstart 1, we presented the process for soloing or muting a track and adjusting its volume. The track menu (shown in Figure 5.7) provides another means of accomplishing these tasks for a selected track. This menu is more useful if adjustments need to be made to these settings while in Instrument Performance and Settings view (rather than Track View).

Edit Track Panning

The Track Pan setting found in this menu is for the purposes of placing the track more in the left or right speaker of the stereo mix. For those listening, this gives the impression that the instrument may be located more on the left, right, or center of the ensemble. It is a common practice to place lead instruments (vocals or melodies) and essential instruments (such as bass and drums) near the center, while placing other instruments slightly to the left or right—although there are no hard-and-fast rules about how this should be done. Often, you can obtain a clearer overall sound by adjusting the panning settings.

Edit Echo and Reverb

The remaining settings in the track menu apply echo and reverb effects to the selected track or to the master track (see the menus and submenus in Figures 5.8 through 5.10).

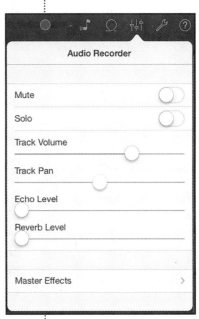

Figure 5.7 GarageBand track menu.

Echo is a repeat of the track, and there are numerous types of echo built into GarageBand: Ambient Delay, Dance Echo A, Dark Eighth Note Echo, and so on. Experiment with these to find the desired effect.

Reverb is a similar effect to echo, but it generally includes a pattern of echos, as might be found in a specific room or performance space. Again, different of types of reverb are built into GarageBand, including Ambience, Cathedral, Chamber, and so on. You can experiment to find the desired echo and reverb for the individually selected track and for the master track (all tracks; see Figure 5.10).

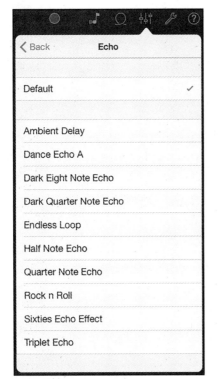

Figure 5.8 Echo submenu.

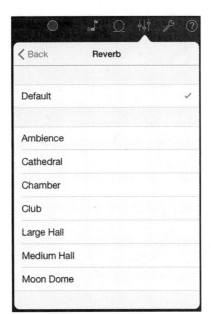

Figure 5.9 Reverb submenu.

Figure 5.10 Master Effects submenu.

Automatic Fade-Outs

In popular music, sometimes it's common to write no ending at all, but to repeat a section and fade out. If you turn on this setting, GarageBand will fade the master track volume of the last four measures of the song from full to nothing. While this ending may work with the last four measures of a song, it is a common practice to add four additional measures for the fade. Those four measures may be any four that are musically satisfying. For example, if the last section of the music is the chorus of a song, four measures from the beginning of the chorus may be used. In some cases, it may work better to simply repeat the last four-measure phrase for the fade-out. You can select the material through looping or split-copy-and-paste operations.

GarageBand for iOS doesn't permit any variations on its default fade-out behavior. If the fade-out sounds good, then it is an option for the ending. Otherwise, you may need to write a more convincing musical ending.

NOTE: If there are empty measures at the end of a song, the fade-out may appear to do nothing. Set the song length appropriately for the desired fade-out.

Chapter 6: Editing MIDI

In Quickstart Chapter 2, we introduced the concept of two different kinds of tracks: digital audio tracks and MIDI tracks. As mentioned before, the two are easily distinguished in GarageBand because digital audio tracks are blue and MIDI tracks are green. Digital audio tracks contain audio recordings of actual instruments, while MIDI tracks contain notes that are to be played on an electronic instrument. The differences in these tracks are readily apparent when you're editing them. You can split, cut, copy, and paste both types of tracks, and you can apply echo, reverb, and other effects to both types of tracks.

Splitting a Digital Audio or MIDI Track

Once a digital audio or MIDI track has been recorded, you can split it into sections.

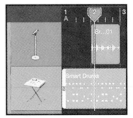

Figure 6.1 Playhead at the location of the split.

1. Position the playhead where you would like to split the track (see Figure 6.1).

2. Double-tap a track and select Split from the menu that appears, as shown in Figure 6.2.

Figure 6.2 Split menu option.

3. When the scissors appear, as shown in Figure 6.3, slide them down across the track to be split. The track will be split as shown in Figure 6.4.

Figure 6.3 The scissors allowing you to split a track.

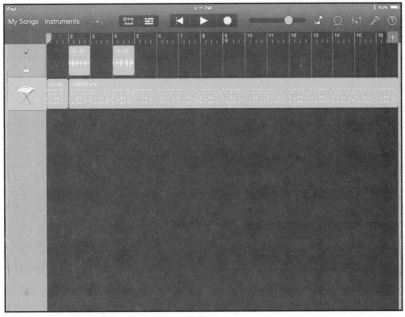

Figure 6.4 The newly split track.

Once a track is split, you can select either side of it with a double-tap and then apply the standard editing operations, such as Cut, Copy, Delete, Loop, Split, Join, and Rename.

Joining a MIDI Track

In Figures 6.5 and 6.6, two sections of music have been selected, double-tapped, and joined.

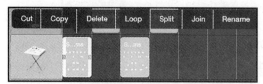

Figure 6.5 Join menu option.

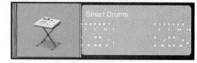

Figure 6.6 Two joined tracks.

Note: The Join option is available for MIDI touch instruments but not for digital audio tracks in current versions of GarageBand for iOS.

Looping a Digital Audio or MIDI Track

Often in music, it is appropriate to play repeated patterns. This is especially true in contemporary drumset music, but sometimes in other music as well. In Pachelbel's "Canon in D," the cello player repeats the same eight notes approximately 30 times.

To loop a section in GarageBand, select the desired section and double-tap it. Choose Loop, and that section of music will be extended to fill the available time. If the loop is too long or too short, you can drag the right side of the loop to the desired length. See Figures 6.7 and 6.8.

Figure 6.7 Loop menu option.

Figure 6.8 The newly created looped section.

Specific MIDI Editing Techniques

The distinguishing characteristic of MIDI tracks is that you can edit them note by note. You can correct or delete wrong notes, and you can add missing notes. You can improve imprecise rhythms manually or automatically. You can change note durations, and you can edit strong or weak attacks. You can fine-tune articulations, and you can adjust MIDI controllers, such as pedal markings. See Figure 6.9 for an image of digital audio and MIDI tracks in GarageBand for iOS.

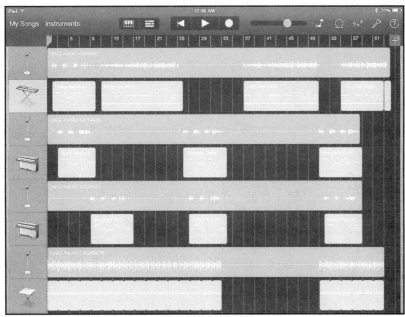

Figure 6.9 Digital audio and MIDI in GarageBand for iOS.

To begin editing a MIDI track, double-tap it and select Edit from the menu that appears. Bubbles like the ones shown in Figure 6.10 will appear.

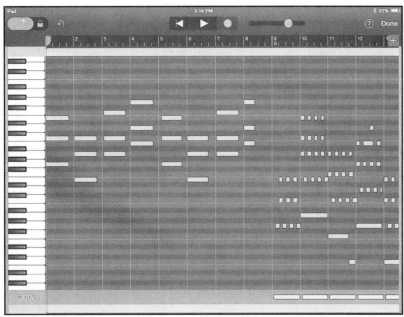

Figure 6.10 MIDI bubbles.

Press the Play button to begin listening to the notes. Your ears and eyes will help you identify incorrect notes. When you've located an incorrect note, double-tap it to delete it (choose Delete from the menu that appears) or drag it to the correct pitch. The note will play as you drag it, so your ear will help you know when it is correct.

If there is a missing note, tap the Pencil tool in the upper-left corner and tap where the note should be. The keyboard to the left of the screen will help you identify the correct location of notes; and again, notes will sound as they are entered. See Figure 6.11.

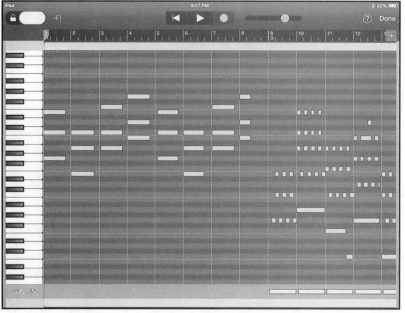

Figure 6.11 Tap to add or delete MIDI notes.

If a note is not on the beat, you can drag it (from the left side of the bubble) to start on that beat. If a note is too short or too long, you can drag it (from the right side of the bubble) to lengthen or shorten it. When you're dragging notes from the left, they snap to the grid of eighth or quarter notes as reflected by the lines. If you would prefer to drag the notes without them snapping to the grid, you must zoom out until no lines are visible. Repeatedly do a reverse pinch of the screen until GarageBand reaches its maximum zoom value.

Editing Multiple Notes

Sometimes, a passage may be too soft, and you might want to make a group of notes louder. Drag a box around the notes to be edited and double-tap one of them. The menu that appears will have a Velocity option, as shown in Figure 6.12. Select it, and a velocity slider will appear (see Figure 6.13). Move the slider right or left to adjust the volume of all of the selected notes up or down.

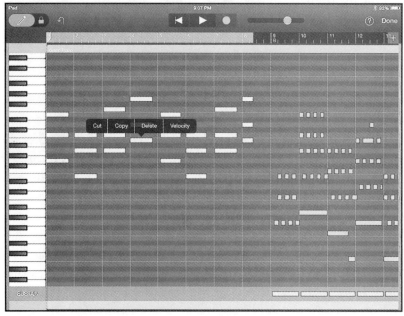

Figure 6.12 Drag to select notes and then choose Velocity.

Figure 6.13 Velocity slider allows you to make a mass velocity adjustment.

You can also reposition all selected notes by dragging them left or right to better align with the beats, and you can transpose them by dragging them up or down to a new octave or to a new key.

If there is pedal-controller information in the track, it will appear at the bottom of the screen, as shown in Figure 6.14. You can edit these pedal markings as you would other MIDI data. Double-tap them and choose from the options that appear, or drag the bubbles to adjust their rhythmic starting and stopping.

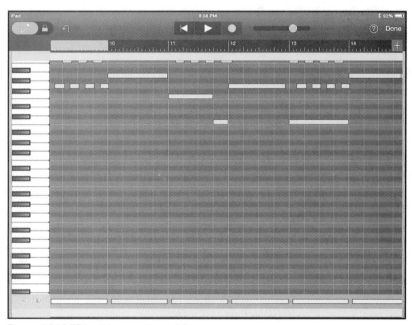

Figure 6.14 MIDI editing: sustain pedal.

Although it has been mentioned before, the Undo tool is especially useful when editing MIDI. As soon as an edit appears to have done something differently than expected, it's good to use the Undo tool, and try again. See Figure 6.15.

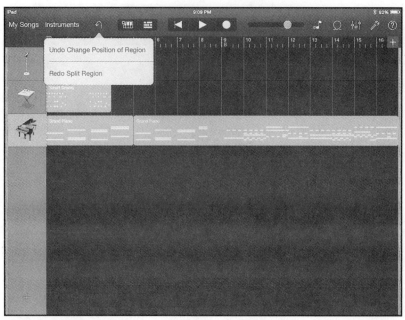

Figure 6.15 MIDI editing: Undo option.

Quantizing Notes

Sometimes when you're recording or importing MIDI data, it turns out that the notes don't align well with the beats. You can apply quantization to a group of selected MIDI notes to adjust incorrect rhythms automatically.

Because quantization moves the notes' attacks to the nearest portion of the beat, quantizing can sometimes have a "stiffening" effect on the music, making it too perfect or "too square." For that reason, quantizing is suggested only for portions of music where the rhythmic errors would produce a greater negative effect than a stiff section. If notes are okay without quantization, it's best to leave them alone.

To quantize notes, do the following:

1. Select the desired notes. You can do this in MIDI Edit view, or you can select an entire section of data in Track view. The former is recommended.

2. From the track menu (see Figure 6.16), select Quantize.

3. Choose the value by which rhythmic errors should be adjusted (see Figure 6.17). Note that there are straight, triplet, and swing options for quantization. Choose the style based on the type of music in the section to be quantized. Applying swing quantization changes straight eighth notes so that they swing, and vice versa.

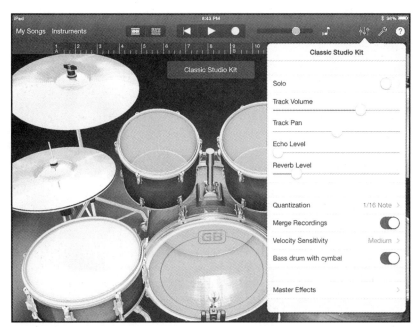

Figure 6.16 Quantization option.

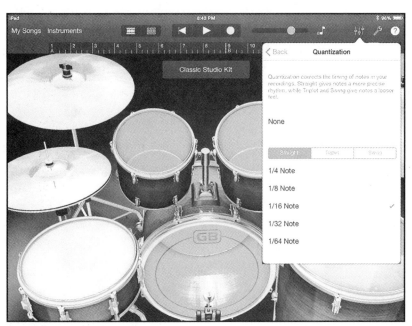

Figure 6.17 Quantization menu.

Chapter 7: GarageBand Guitar Effects

Most guitarists who play an electric instrument own an amplifier that enhances its sound and effects pedals that provide further options. A great strength of GarageBand for Mac and for iOS is its variety of amplifiers and effects processors (boxes) you can apply to live performance or to recorded tracks.

GarageBand for iOS currently has four categories of amplifiers: clean, crunchy, distorted, and processed. The clean amplifiers have a relatively pure guitar sound, primarily with some equalization that darkens or warms the sound. The crunchy guitars have overdrive applied so that the sound has a strong attack. Distorted guitars often have a much higher level of gain saturation mixed with their tone. Processed guitars have vibrato, tremolo, or other effects added.

As of this writing, GarageBand for iOS has 10 effects pedals. See the "GarageBand Effects Boxes" section at the end of this chapter for brief explanation of each.

Playing Live Guitar Using GarageBand Effects

To hear the effects of the GarageBand for iOS amplifiers on live performance, you must connect your guitar to an input on the iPad and from a GarageBand song, create a track using the Guitar Amp instrument (see Figure 7.1).

Figure 7.1 Instrument Selection view: Guitar Amp.

The easiest way to connect your guitar to the iPad is through a device such as the iRig Guitar or iRig PRO. (See Chapter 10) Plug the iRig into the iPad, and plug the 1/4-inch cable from the guitar into the iRig. The iRig Guitar uses the iPad's Line In input to send the signal into the iPad and should produce good results. The iRig PRO sends the signal of the guitar into the 30-pin USB port through the Apple Camera Connection Kit and should give excellent results.

You can also use any standard USB Core Audio interface with 1/4-inch guitar inputs that is plugged into the iPad through the Apple Camera Connection Kit. This approach will also yield excellent results. (See Chapter 10.)

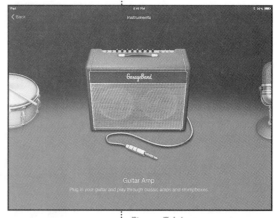

Figure 7.2 Clean Combo guitar amp.

Finally, the iPad's output, probably through the headphone jack, must be sent to an amplifier (or headphones or earbuds). You might need to tap GarageBand's plug button in the upper-left corner of the iPad screen and turn monitoring on so that the guitar amp plays through the headphone jack of your iOS device.

When these connections are in place, start playing. The default Clean Combo amp will be playing (see Figure 7.2). You can adjust the controls on each amp to customize the sound if you desire. Also, each amp includes at least one effects box. Click the effects box icon at the top right of the screen to see which effects are applied to the amp. Click the label of the amp to choose another.

GarageBand for iOS currently has 32 amplifiers from which to choose, as shown in Figures 7.3 through 7.6. Select an amp that matches the style of music being played.

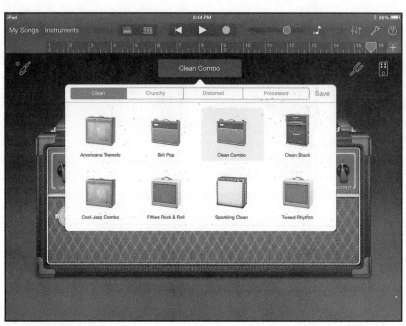

Figure 7.3 Clean amps.

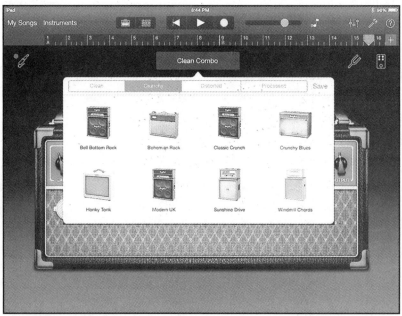

Figure 7.4 Crunchy amps.

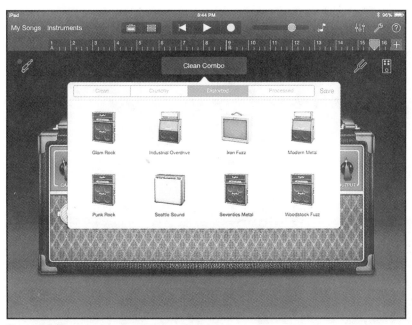

Figure 7.5 Distorted amps.

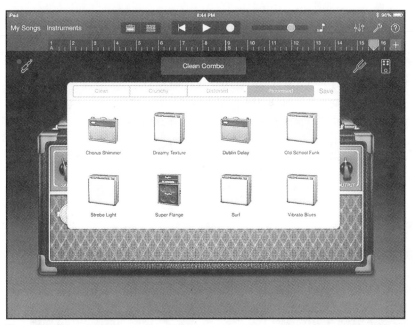

Figure 7.6 Processed amps.

If you would like to edit or add "box" effects to the amp sound, click on the box icon on the top right of the amp screen. Something like Figure 7.7 will appear. Adjust the settings on these pedals, tap the empty pedal slot to select other pedals to use, or drag the pedals to rearrange their order. As of this writing, GarageBand for iOS has 10 effects pedals.

Figure 7.7 Guitar effects pedals.

Almost every guitarist's pedal collection includes one or more pedals devoted to tuning. GarageBand places the tuner front and center. Tap on the tuning fork and play a note. If the note is perfectly in tune, it will light in blue (see Figure 7.8). If it is sharp or flat, the amount will be reflected on the lines to the left or right of the note. Click the tuning fork again when you're finished tuning to resume playing.

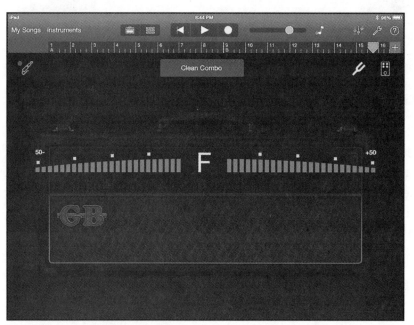

Figure 7.8 Guitar tuner.

Applying GarageBand Effects to Recorded Guitar Tracks

Although you can apply GarageBand amp and pedal effects to live guitar performances, their greatest use is in recording. You can record a clean guitar sound and then experiment with new amps and pedal combinations. Often, you can achieve good results that make a greater musical impact in this manner.

GarageBand Effects Boxes

All GarageBand effects boxes have an equivalent family of hardware pedals on which they are based. All also have adjustable settings. Often, those settings permit enhancements to the sound that go beyond their primary functions. Experimenting with the various settings is the only way to learn what is possible with these pedals.

- **Squash Compressor.** Keeps the loud and soft signals from the guitar from being too far apart.

- **Blue Echo.** Provides a fairly universal echo delay effect.

- **Phase Tripper.** Adds a bit of edge to the sound in a manner that may include some light vibrato.

- **Vintage Drive.** Provides an overdrive effect similar to some amplifiers.

- **Hi Drive.** Provides an equalization boost of higher frequencies.

- **Fuzz Machine.** Adds a "fuzzy" distortion to the sound to thicken the texture.

- **Heavenly Chorus.** Thickens the texture by adding slightly modified copies of the same signal.

- **Robo Flanger.** Adds edge to the sound, similar to the phaser.

- **The Vibe.** Adds vibrato.

- **Auto Funk.** Adds a custom effect attempting to imitate a "funk" guitar sound (similar to a mix of phaser, fuzz, and wah).

Chapter 8: Transferring Files to and from Your Mac and iOS Device

The Quickstart chapters earlier in the book demonstrated how to open and play songs that were created on the iPad. Additionally, you learned to save songs you created to GarageBand's song list and to share songs created on the iPad through email, YouTube, and SoundCloud.

This chapter will cover the details of using Apple's iTunes file-sharing system for copying songs to and from the iPad. The reasons why you would want to do this are as follows.

- **Files from iOS to Mac:** To take a song or project started on the iPad to GarageBand or Logic on the Mac for additional editing.

- **Files from Mac to iOS:** To load, play, and edit the song files developed by others on your iPad. Other iOS GarageBand song sources include songs developed for this book; songs developed by friends, classmates, and other GarageBand users; and songs from the Internet.

The iTunes file-sharing option is useful for copying specific file types to and from GarageBand for iOS. You can copy GarageBand source files (.band) from your iOS device to your Mac for further editing. You can also copy GarageBand iOS source files from your Mac to your iOS device for further editing, but you must take care to copy only GarageBand iOS files. Finally, you can copy sound files in a variety of formats from your Mac to your iOS device. Those sound files are most commonly .caf, .wav, .mp3, .aif, and .mp4. GarageBand for iOS can use these sound files in its songs as loops and as sounds for its sampler.

Transferring Files from iOS to Mac

There are basically two main steps in the process of transferring GarageBand iOS files to the Mac.

STEP 1

From the iOS device, do the following:

1. From GarageBand for iOS, go to the project list. (Tap My Songs if necessary.)

2. Click Select (or Edit in previous versions of GarageBand for iOS).

3. Select a song to send to GarageBand.

4. Tap the Share button.

5. Click the iTunes icon to send it to iTunes.

6. When you're presented with a choice of sending the song as an iTunes file or as a GarageBand project file, choose the GarageBand option.

7. Connect your iPad and Mac using the appropriate cable. You don't usually need to sync the iPad, but it may do so automatically.

STEP 2

Then, from your Mac, do the following:

1. From iTunes on the Mac, click the icon for the iOS device (see Figure 8.1).

Figure 8.1 iTunes iOS device list.

Figure 8.2 iTunes iOS device Apps tab.

2. Click on the Apps tab near the top of the screen, as shown in Figure 8.2.

3. Scroll to the bottom of the screen, where the list of file-sharing apps is located. Click GarageBand and, in the list that appears, look for the file sent from the iPad (see Figure 8.3).

Figure 8.3 iTunes file sharing—GarageBand for iOS.

Figure 8.4 iTunes file-sharing options.

4. Drag that file onto the desktop or into an appropriate document folder (or click the file and choose Save To from the bottom of the window, as shown in Figure 8.4).

5. Navigate to the file from the computer's OS, and double-click it to open it in GarageBand on your Mac. The Mac will make a copy in an updated format for the Mac. It may display a prompt for a filename. It's best not to overwrite the original GarageBand for iOS file, because you can still share that one with iOS users. You normally can't take the one updated for the Mac back to GarageBand on an iOS device.

Transferring Files from Mac to iOS

Again, there are basically two steps in transferring files from your Mac to GarageBand for iOS. This is roughly the reverse of the process described a moment ago, but it is presented here with an explanation of any differences. It is important to note that when you're going from the Mac to iOS, you can transfer only GarageBand files for iOS. If you attempt to transfer GarageBand files for Mac, the iOS device will typically refuse to open them.

STEP 1

From your Mac, do the following:

1. Connect your iPad and Mac using a cable. You don't usually need to sync your iPad, but the process may start automatically.

2. From iTunes on your Mac, click the icon for the iOS device.

3. Click on the Apps tab near the top of the screen.

4. Scroll to the bottom of the screen where the list of file-sharing apps is located. Click GarageBand to see the files—if any—that have previously been shared between the Mac and the iPad.

5. Locate the file from your Mac that you wish to send to GarageBand for iOS and drag that file into this list (or click the Add button from the bottom of the window). If the file exists already, it may prompt you to overwrite it. Because of the different versions of the GarageBand files required for iOS and for the Mac, it's a good idea to be clear about it before answering yes.

STEP 2

Then, from your iOS device, do the following:

1. From GarageBand for iOS, go to the project list. (Tap My Songs if necessary.)

2. Click the + button.

3. Choose Copy from iTunes File Sharing, as shown in Figure 8.5.

4. Scroll through the list and select the song sent from the Mac (see Figure 8.6). Only GarageBand for iOS files will appear. GarageBand files for Mac will be displayed in gray and cannot be selected. The song will be copied to the GarageBand for iOS song list. From there, it may be opened and edited.

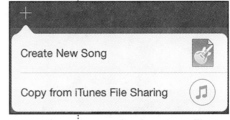

Figure 8.5 Copy from iTunes File-Sharing option.

Figure 8.6 GarageBand Copy from iTunes File Sharing—song selection menu.

There is at least one additional way to get songs from your Mac to your iOS device that may be easier. You can email a GarageBand for iOS file from your email client on your Mac to your email on the iOS device. However, note that this may not work in all versions of GarageBand for iOS.

To do so, from the Mac, email a GarageBand for iOS file to yourself. Then, in your email program on your iPad, click and hold the attachment. Choose Open in GarageBand when the option appears. This will work only if the song is small enough to make the email journey.

Two additional file transfer methods from Apple deserve consideration: iCloud and AirDrop.

iCloud

Specifically, if you are working on GarageBand on one iOS device (such as your iPhone) and you wish to send it to GarageBand on another iOS device on the same iCloud account (such as your iPad), you can do so through iCloud. This is done through the song list screen, as illustrated in Figures 8.7 through 8.9. To send a song to iCloud, select it in the songlist, tap the iCloud icon in GarageBand's menu, and select, "Send to iCloud." An icon will be added to the song's icon to show that it is saved in the cloud. To remove a song from the cloud, repeat the process selecting a file with the iCloud icon, and choose, Remove from iCloud.

This method only works from one iOS device to another. There's currently not a way to move a file from iCloud to your Mac. Perhaps in the future that will also be supported. The iCloud method of transferring files could be especially helpful to teachers whose entire collection of iPads uses the same iCloud account.

Figure 8.7 Upload Song to iCloud option.

Figure 8.8 iCloud icon.

Figure 8.9 Remove Song from iCloud option.

AirDrop

AirDrop requires Bluetooth and Wi-Fi be turned on and only works on suitably powerful iOS devices, such as the iPhone 5 or later, the fourth-generation iPad, the iPad mini, and the fifth-generation iPod Touch. You can use AirDrop on iOS only to share files with other iOS devices. Mac users cannot use AirDrop to share files with iOS users, and iOS users cannot use AirDrop to share files with Mac computers.

Amidst all these restrictions is some good news. GarageBand 2.0 supports the transfer of files by AirDrop. If your system meets the criteria, then AirDrop may be an option for you. According to Apple, to use AirDrop, you must turn it on in the Control Center on both the sending and the receiving machine. From GarageBand on the receiving machine, navigate to the Song List view, select a song, and press the Share button. AirDrop will be an option. The receiving machine should now accept the file.

Search Apple's Support Site for more information.

Other File-Sharing Options

A few file-sharing services offer some potential for exchanging data. Most popular are Dropbox and Box.com. Both services offer free accounts, and in both cases you get a generous initial amount of storage space.

One great advantage is that once you've uploaded your files to your storage space, you can then use those files on any computer or iPad with an Internet connection. You don't have to worry about copying the files using flash drives or other media.

Another great advantage is that instead of attempting to send large files through email, you can put them in your online storage and then share a link to them by email. It saves space on email servers and increases the reliability of the transfer of large files.

Both of these services have free apps that permit you to view your saved files from your iOS device, so the potential for their use by iOS apps should be great. In fact, if you are working with commonly used digital audio file formats (tracks to be imported into your GarageBand for iOS projects or for files created by projects that you have completed in GarageBand for iOS), these services work well.

The one area where these services do *not* do well is in the storage and transfer of GarageBand source files. As of this writing, there is no easy way to transfer GarageBand source files from the iOS device directly to these services, or to transfer GarageBand source files from these services to GarageBand for iOS. Until this problem is solved, iTunes file sharing is the most reliable means of moving GarageBand source files.

Summary

Historically, users of GarageBand for iOS have been able to save their song files in their own space on the iPad (in the song list in GarageBand). Those files, however, were available only to that iOS device. To get GarageBand for iOS files from an iPad to a Mac requires the use of iTunes file-sharing features.

While it is possible to share GarageBand for iOS files to a Mac, open them, and edit them, the opposite procedure is not currently supported by Apple. In other words, once a GarageBand for iOS file has been moved to a Mac and opened and edited in GarageBand, that version of the file can no longer be sent to or edited in GarageBand for iOS.

If you do have files on your Mac for GarageBand for iOS, you can send them to the iOS device through iTunes file sharing or through email (if they are small enough for email). File sharing supports larger files. File sharing and email support the transfer of files to machines that are not normally synced with an iPad.

A couple of additional file-sharing options are available from Apple, including iCloud and AirDrop. These work well provided you have an Apple account and your equipment meets the minimum criteria.

File-sharing services such as dropbox.com and box.com also provide a useful service for standard audio files. They are not useful for transferring .band files.

Chapter 9: iPad Performing Ensembles

It is becoming increasingly common for people to organize ensembles of iPad performers. This chapter contains a number of songs that would be appropriate for such a group. These arrangements are designed to be easily played using the instruments in GarageBand, and performing them will help you learn more about music, GarageBand instruments, and music production.

For most songs in this chapter, we've provided the melody and chords. By using GarageBand's smart instruments and the melodies in this chapter, you can create convincing performances of each song.

Using GarageBand's Jam Sessions Feature

If you'll be using multiple smart instruments, a common problem is syncing those instruments with one another. Fortunately, GarageBand offers its Jam Sessions feature, which allows you to use the auto accompanying patterns in sync with one another. See Chapter 11 on Jam Sessions for more information.

Advanced Arrangements

Their are PDF versions of the songs that you can download at _www.alfred. com/LearningGarageBand_. These PDFs will give you the standard notation and arrangements for each of the songs.

Loading a Song into an iPad

You can download the GarageBand for iOS versions of these songs (and their accompaniments, if applicable) from the book's Website (_www.alfred.com/ LearningGarageBand_) and play them on GarageBand 2.0 or higher.

To put these songs on an iPad, follow these five steps. Note: this approach works for .wav files, but not for .band files.

1. From a desktop or laptop computer, go to the book's downloadable assets (_www.alfred.com/LearningGarageBand_) and navigate to the desired song.

2. Right-click the link to the iOS version of the file and download it to your computer.

3. From the desktop or laptop computer, attach the downloaded file to an email and send it to an email address you can check on your iPad.

4. From the iPad, locate the email, and tap and hold on the attached file.

5. From the pop-up menu that appears, choose Open with GarageBand.

Note: If a file is too large for email, use the iTunes file-sharing method described in Chapter 8. To work with .band files, see Chapter 1 and Chapter 8.

Amplification for GarageBand Ensembles

To have a workable iPad ensemble, you must have a workable amplification system for all members of the class. This is especially important for live performance with multiple iPads.

You might be able to do some limited rehearsal of small iPad ensembles using only the speaker on the iPad, but it will be especially hard to hear softer instruments, and combining these with traditional acoustic instruments or singing ensures that the iPad instrument will be virtually inaudible. Sound reinforcement is helpful for rehearsal, but is required for public performance.

The performance options are as follows:

- Multiple iPads plugged into a mixing board and amplification system

- The use of dedicated devices for rehearsing or performing together with electronic instruments

Mixing Board and Amplification

Typically, a small mixing board with eight line-in inputs would handle most iPad ensembles. The headphone jack of the iPad is 1/8-inch, and the line input of most mixers is usually 1/4-inch. A simple 1/8-inch cable with a 1/4-inch adapter would serve to make the connection from the iPad to the mixing board.

Because the people playing the iPads need room, you must have cables that allow them sufficient space. Ideally, iPads and the people playing them would have about three feet of space between them and a good bit of distance to the mixer. Although the line level of the iPad is strong, setup is potentially complicated by cables of 15 feet or longer. (They are subject to loss of signal and interference from radio signals.) It's a good idea to limit each cable to 15 feet. If the distances need to be longer, then a direct box converting the signal to a balanced XLR is recommended. If the mixer is in the back of the auditorium, then direct boxes and XLR cables are a necessity.

Another important component of any ensemble is vocals. Normally, a mixer supports microphone inputs also, and it would be wise to include microphones in a classroom setup.

One commonly used vocal effect in iPad ensembles is the pitch-correction effect, found so often in the music of recording artist T-Pain that it has come to be known as the T-Pain effect. GarageBand does not support this effect, so you'd need to devote another channel in the mixer to an iPad running a T-Pain vocal application. In this case, unless the T-Pain app supports inter-app communication, you'd need to record the output of the mixer instead of an iPad Jam Session. Because of the four-player limit for jam sessions, that would be true of any ensemble of more than four instruments.

You can also use wireless transmitters with iPads, so that performers can move around unencumbered by cables (although they do have to carry transmitter packs, and the sound system has to have enough inputs for the wireless receivers).

The mixer should be controlled by the teacher or a responsible student. The mixer can be analog or digital for performances. Both are easily recorded. The primary advantage of a digital mixer is that it permits layered recording of as many instruments as the mixer supports, but only to a computer. As of this writing, the iPad records only two channels at a time. Be careful to get a multichannel digital mixer for computers. A simple stereo digital mixer would work if you're recording to the iPad, although GarageBand Jam Sessions would be better for up to four instruments.

If there will be multiple iPad ensembles in the same space, then you'd need a group of small mixers placed throughout the room that distribute signals to headphones.

Dedicated Devices for Rehearsing or Performing

You can also purchase audio hubs that connect several students for playing together in rehearsal. You can use these with headphones, so if the ensemble is all iPads (no vocalists or acoustic instruments), players can rehearse with one another with little disturbance to those around them. One advantage of these systems is that they work with other electronic instruments as well, such as electronic guitars, basses, and keyboards.

The mixer or amplification system and rehearsal systems should support the desired number of performers. It may be practical, however, to limit ensembles to a number that can be easily managed with a small mixer (perhaps six or eight performers). The rehearsal hub shown in Figure 9.1 supports six performers, although there are versions of it that support greater numbers.

Figure 9.1 JamHub BedRoom.

Songs for Performance

This section of the book contains songs for performance individually or in a small ensemble. The songs in this book are organized according to the following categories: Decades, Cultures, Folk Music, Events, and Just for Fun.

- **Decades.** The first organization is by decade. The styles of music played by "garage bands" has followed the trends of popular music through the years, so studying these songs provides historical insight into popular music and culture. There is at least one example of a song written in the style of each decade.

- **Cultures.** The world is an increasingly smaller place. Although the scope of this book does not permit examples from every world culture, many are represented.

- **Folk Music.** Every culture has its own music, and those from decidedly non-Western influences are presented in the section on cultures. Within Western music, there are numerous subcultures, and many of those are represented in this section.

- **Events.** We tend to organize our schedules around events such as birthdays and holidays. This section of the chapter presents music for various times of year.

- **Just for Fun.** Some music defies categorization. Those songs are included in this section.

Performance and Activity Suggestions

The following activities are recommended for each song, so these instructions will be referenced below but only the most relevant for each song will be repeated on each page. We covered all skills required to complete these activities in the Quickstart chapters. Review those if necessary.

The following performance and activity suggestions are organized according to the following categories: Performance, Recording, Composition, Listening, and Other.

Performance

- Listen to the song on the iOS device, and if there are lyrics, sing with the provided GarageBand accompaniment.

- Listen to the song on the iOS device, and if there are no lyrics, play the melody with the provided GarageBand accompaniment.

- Turn off the vocal or melodic tracks, and sing or play along with the accompaniment.

- Form an iPad ensemble to play the song.

    ♦ One or more people should play the melody on an instrument appropriate for this style.

    ♦ One or more should play a bass line using a simple rhythm and following the given chords.

- ♦ One or more should play a GarageBand smart instrument using the chords indicated. Create a Jam Session to synchronize more than one smart instrument if necessary.

- ♦ One or more should improvise a drum part.

- Download the PDFs from *www.alfred.com/LearningGarageBand* and play the versions found there. These are categorized as easy, intermediate, or difficult.

Recording

- Lyrics and melodies

  - ♦ If there are lyrics, mute the melody and record yourself singing into a new track. Match the original style or experiment with new styles of singing. Try recording yourself whistling the melody.

  - ♦ If there are no lyrics, mute the melody and record yourself playing it into a new track. Match the original style or experiment with new instruments.

  - ♦ Mute the various tracks and replace them with your performances. Try to match the style of the original. You will learn a lot about music and GarageBand by recording each track.

  - ♦ Find a guitar track and use GarageBand's guitar effects to add overdrive or other effects to the recorded guitar.

- Composition

  - ♦ Write and record new lyrics and record yourself singing them. Match the original style. Mute the original voice.

  - ♦ Create and record a spoken rap that could accompany the song. Mute the original voice or melody.

  - ♦ Improvise a new melody. If there are lyrics, you can use the same words, create new ones, or use nonsense syllables (scooby, doo, wah, dot, dah, bah, doot). Mute the original voice or melody.

  - ♦ Duplicate a song and use GarageBand's original instruments (not smart instruments—or use the smart instruments in note mode) to create a new track to replace the original.

  - ♦ Duplicate a song and use GarageBand's smart instruments to create a new and different accompaniment for a given melody. In this case, experiment with different styles of music for the given melody.

  - ♦ Create a theme and variations for a selected song (duplicate the original song, select all and copy it to the end of the song, change the original version).

  - ♦ Rerecord tracks playing new variations live.

- Edit MIDI tracks, creating new variations.

  - ♦ Change the mode from major to minor or vice versa.

  - ♦ Change the melody to include different notes or rhythms.

  - ♦ Change the chords harmonizing a song.

♦ Slice, cut, and paste digital audio and MIDI tracks into new arrangements.

♦ Open several of the provided GarageBand songs. Find one that is quiet and subdued. Create a custom arrangement, building as much energy as possible into the performance. One strategy is to use drums from GarageBand's loops, which provide more energy. Another is to rerecord vocal tracks with additional energy.

♦ Using only GarageBand loops, create your own rondo in ABACABA form.

♦ Write your own pentatonic song. Use either a major (C–D–E–G–A) or a minor (C–D–E♭–G–A♭) scale.

• Listening

♦ Open a provided GarageBand song and listen to it. List the instruments used.

♦ Open a provided GarageBand song and change the instruments that are used to play each voice (if permitted—this will not work with digital audio tracks and some MIDI tracks). Experiment with replacing natural instruments with electronic ones, and vice versa.

• Listen to the provided GarageBand accompaniment and describe the unique features of the song.

♦ Melody: Is it diatonic, pentatonic, or other? How is it sung or played?

♦ Harmony: Is it consonant or dissonant, major or minor? Describe tension and resolution, if applicable.

♦ Rhythm: What are the time signature and tempo? Do the eighth notes swing or are they played evenly? What are other unique rhythmic features?

♦ Form: Describe the sections found in the piece. Make a formal map of the song. Describe repetition and contrast. If the song uses variation techniques, describe them. If the song uses a familiar form (verse-chorus, AB, rondo), describe it.

♦ Expression: Describe dynamics, tempos, and articulations of the piece. Describe the techniques used to build the song.

♦ What distinguishes this song stylistically from other songs in the book?

♦ Listen to the various voices in the piece (drums, guitar, bass, keys). On the music in the book, mark the measures where they play.

Other Activities

• Download additional sounds to the iPad and create an arrangement that features that sound file. For example, for "Old MacDonald," download farm-animal sounds and use them in the song.

• Record a sound into GarageBand's sampler and create a composition featuring the recorded instrument.

Music by the Decades

Popular music changes quickly, and each decade has its own character. The following songs are written in a style that is consistent with the music of that decade. In some cases, a specific song may come to mind, but the intent is to capture the general style characteristics of each decade.

1940s

In the years before television, radio was the primary medium through which people experienced music. Because of radio's influence, the 1940s are remembered for the swing music of the big bands, but live performance was also healthy. This section will present a 12-bar blues piece, a style of music commonly performed by live groups, and a swing piece played by a small jazz combo.

"Blues"

ACTIVITY:

This song is from the book's digital files and is labeled 01-Blues.band. This version is an instrumental song.

The blues arose in the Mississippi Delta region. This song is a literal version of the 12-bar blues, a common version based on the following chords. You can transpose these chords to different keys as necessary.

C7, C7, C7, C7, F7, F7, C7, C7, G7, F7, C7, C7

As implied by the name, the lyrics to the blues were often about the difficult circumstances of life, but there is seldom complete despair, as hope is a major characteristic of the people from whom the blues arose.

Improvisation was common over the 12-bar blues. In this recording, the first 12 bars have only the accompaniment, and there are three additional times through the progression, each time with a guitar solo as shown in the music.

Performance and activity suggestions:

- See the notes at the beginning of this chapter.

- Play along with this recording and improvise during the 12-bar introduction the second time through, or mute the tracks with the solo and improvise freely throughout.

- Create an ensemble and play the music for the rhythm section (guitar, piano, bass, drums) for this song from the book's downloadable PDF files. In the arrangement, the melody is played by two instruments in a call-and-response fashion.

"At the Beach"

ACTIVITY:

This song is from the book's digital files and is labeled 02-At_The_Beach.band.

This piece is based on a variation of the 12-bar blues and is sung with a strong blues style. In the traditional 12-bar blues, there would be 12 bars between the repeats. In this version, the two-measure G7 and F7 pattern is repeated, and the closing chord of the lyrics is extended by two measures to give a 16-bar variation. Among the chord progressions that have impacted music, few have had the influence of the 12-bar blues. Although all of the notes are written for this song, a key feature of blues and jazz is improvisation, where the performer might repeat the chord progressions, sing or play variations of the melody, and make up new melodies.

Performance and activity suggestions:

- See the notes at the beginning of this chapter.

- Mute the voice and improvise a new melody. Use the same words or make up nonsense syllables (scooby, doo, wah, and so on).

- Play the arrangement found in the online score at *www.alfred.com/ LearningGarageBand*. The right hand of the piano part is often marked two octaves higher, but it works in any octave as written and higher.

- This song has a verse section, starting with "Come on down" and a chorus part starting with "At the Beach." In the recording, the verse and chorus are repeated twice. Write a second verse and record it.

"We Can Swing"

ACTIVITY:

This song is from the book's digital files and is labeled 03-We_Can_Swing.band .

In the 1940s, swing music was popular. Although the iPad does not currently play all big-band instruments (trumpets, saxophones, and so on), it can swing. This song uses a 1940s swing style with a small swing combo (combination of instruments).

Performance and activity suggestions:

- Refer to the notes at the beginning of this chapter.

- Play the arrangement found online.

- This song has five rehearsal letters. A, B, and C are different. D is the same as C with a thicker texture, and E is the same as A. Extend the song, and repeat A between each section to form a Rondo.

- Open a different song that contains only MIDI tracks (for example, song 22, "Country Dogs"), and turn the swing-style quantization on from the tools menu on each track. Listen to the song before and after, and describe the difference. Experiment with different settings.

1950s

The 1950s saw the rise of commercial television. Musically, there were three especially notable trends: doo wop, Elvis Presley, and the formation of The Beatles, although some of their greatest influence was in the next decade. This book will focus on the doo wop music of this era.

"Doo Wop Triplets"

ACTIVITY:

This song is from the book's digital files and is labeled 04-Doo_Wop_Triplets.band.

Many types of music were popular in the 1950s (Elvis, The Beatles, and so on), but one type that was particularly popular was doo wop. It was very common for doo wop songs to use a repeating chord progression like the following (transposed to different keys as needed): C–Am–F–G. It was also common for some instruments to play specific figures. In this piece, the doo wop chords are used, and the piano plays triplets in a manner that was very common.

Performance and activity suggestions:

- Refer to the notes at the beginning of this chapter.

- Play the arrangement found online.

- This song begins with an introduction, followed by three rehearsal letters. A, B, and C are all different. Which is more like a chorus, and which is more like a verse? Which could serve as an instrumental or "bridge?" Copy and paste the song to extend it and arrange it in a typical song form (verse, chorus, verse, chorus, instrumental/bridge, chorus).

"Doo Wop Guitar"

ACTIVITY:

This song is from the book's digital files and is labeled 05-Doo_Wop_Guitar.band.

This doo wop song uses the same chords as the previous one, but without the piano and with a very different guitar feel.

Performance and activity suggestions:

- See the notes at the beginning of this chapter.

- Create a new audio track, and record a vocal version of the instrumental solo.

- The song begins with an introduction of four measures, followed by eight measures that would be typical of a verse, and eight measures that would be typical of a chorus. Copy and paste to extend the song.

1960s

The 1960s saw the continuing popularity of The Beatles and other artists. Other innovative artists, such as James Brown, also contributed to the musical landscape. The music of the day developed a subcultural context often aimed at improving society from the perspective of the artists. Mainstream music, however, focused on themes that have been popular through all decades: enjoying life, having fun, and experiencing love and relationships. The rock music of the day developed more energy. This section will present a rock tune with strong 1960s influence.

"Feelin' Great"

ACTIVITY:

This song is from the book's digital files and is labeled 06-Feelin_Great.band.

The track features 1960s-style guitar and a bold vocal. This type of rock sound was just arising in the 1960s.

Performance and activity suggestions:

- Review the notes at the beginning of this chapter.

- Measures 1–8 make the chorus of this song, and measures 9–16 the verse. The second half of the song uses the same lyrics. Compose and record new lyrics for verse two.

- Play the arrangement found online.

1970s

The 1970s saw many parallel developments of musical style. There was a light popular music that appealed to a broad audience, concurrent with classic rock and rhythm and blues. The late 1970s saw the rise of dance music, which was then called *disco*. This section will present a light rock ballad and a song in the classic rock style of the 1970s.

In the 1970s, a great emphasis on incorporating new sounds into music was common. Although the electric guitar was invented in the 1930s and became a commonly used instrument in pop music of the 1950s and 1960s, the proliferation of effects pedals and a maturing understanding of how to use overdrive and distortion characterizes much of the music of the 1970s.

"Better Now"

ACTIVITY:

This song is from the book's digital files and is labeled 07-Better_Now.band.

"Better Now" uses sounds and chords made popular in the classic rock of the 1970s. It is in two sections—a slower section at first, and then a more energetic section. The song is instrumental only.

Performance and activity suggestions:

- See the notes at the beginning of this chapter.

- This song has a verse (measures 1–10) and chorus section (measure 11 to the end). Copy and paste each to expand the form. Make the verses quieter than the chorus, but build the song to the end, through the addition of more active parts, especially drums.

- Write and record lyrics for this instrumental song.

"Something in My Eyes"

ACTIVITY:

This song is from the book's digital files and is labeled 08-Something_in_My_Eyes.band.

This one is a classic 1970s ballad. Although the 1970s were known for many styles, light ballads were common. GarageBand's smart guitar has a picking pattern that fits this style well.

Performance and activity suggestions:

- Review the notes at the beginning of this chapter.

- This song begins with an introduction of 12 measures, then a verse of eight measures and a chorus of four measures. Copy and paste the various sections of this song to expand the form. Add drums to make the second chorus more energetic.

- Write and record lyrics for this instrumental song.

1980s

The 1980s saw many parallel developments of musical style. There was again a light popular music that appealed to a broad audience, concurrent with various other strains of music. Many of the ballad styles of previous decades continued. Dance music gained a significant influence in the 1980s. The disco music of the late 1970s began to transform through the innovations of various artists, and new names for these styles developed. Rap was a term used to describe music where a story was told over strongly rhythmic music. Hip-hop combined rap and melodic dance traditions. This section presents three 1980s pieces—one in a popular ballad style and two with hip-hop influence.

Like a Ballerina

ACTIVITY:

This song is from the book's digital files and is labeled 09-Like_A_Ballerina.band.

"Like a Ballerina" uses a classical piano sound and lyrics about a ballerina to establish a quiet, reflective mood.

Performance and activity suggestions:

- Refer to the notes at the beginning of this chapter.

- This song repeats a verse and chorus twice. Write and record new lyrics for verse two.

- Use GarageBand's smart instruments to create a substitute accompaniment.

"I Just Want to Say"

ACTIVITY:

This song is from the book's digital files and is labeled 10-I_Just_Want_To_Say.band.

Here, a techno beat is used to establish a different type of dance feel.

Performance and activity suggestions:

- Review the notes at the beginning of this chapter.

- Rerecord the vocals of this piece with your voice. Use a dreamy sound and lots of reverb.

- Play the arrangement found online.

"Hip-Hop Dance"

ACTIVITY:

This song is from the book's digital files and is labeled 11-Hip_Hop_Dance.band.

In the 1980s, electronic keyboards were very popular. Many of their electronic sounds caught on with those writing dance music. Mix in some R&B cultural roots, and the result is hip-hop.

Performance and activity suggestions:

- Read the notes at the beginning of this chapter.

- Create a rap that could accompany this song and record yourself singing it.

- This song is composed using GarageBand loops. The music is for the bass only. The bass plays the same line throughout.

1990s

Like all decades, many concurrent styles were occurring in the 1990s. One of the most prevalent was love songs of female ballad artists, such as Whitney Houston, Mariah Carey, and Madonna.

"Love Is Forever"

ACTIVITY:

This song is from the book's digital files and is labeled 12-Love_is_Forever.band.

In the 1990s, numerous female artists were singing love ballads. This instrumental song is typical of that style.

Performance and activity suggestions:

- See the notes at the beginning of this chapter.

- This song begins with an introduction of 10 measures, followed by five rehearsal letters. Letter A is the chorus. Letter B is an interlude and Letter C is the verse. Letter D is the chorus again. Just before letter E, the song modulates to the key of D, and letter E contains material suitable for the ending. Add drums and more active accompaniments to give letters D and E more energy.

2000s

As with all decades, many styles were popular in the 2000s. The love songs of female ballad artists like Christina Aguilera, Alicia Keys, Janet Jackson, Jennifer Lopez, and Beyoncé continued, although in many unique styles. One interesting development in the late 1990s and continuing into the 2000s was the rise of the "boy bands," such as 'N Sync and The Backstreet Boys, who sang a light, popular style. There was also an ongoing influence of hip-hop and other dance music. The piece typical of the 2000s presented in this section is "American Techno." The sounds heard in this piece are found in the music of many artists from the 2000s.

"American Techno"

ACTIVITY:

This song is from the book's digital files and is labeled 13-American_Techno.band.

This piece is instrumental only, in a techno dance style.

The time signature in this song is $\frac{4}{4}$, however, the melody often divides the measures into groups of two and three eighth notes (measures 1–8 and 13–14). This is performed against evenly grouped eighth notes in the bass and drums.

Performance and activity suggestions:

- Listen to this song on the iPad and play along.

- Form an iPad ensemble to play this song. Have one person play the melody on an instrument appropriate for this style, one person play a bass line using a simple rhythm, and one person improvise a drum part. Use a Jam Session to synchronize more than one smart instrument if necessary.

- The upper voice works well played two octaves down and with GarageBand's lead synthesizer sounds.

- The lower voice works well played as written with GarageBand's keyboard bass sounds. Play the two parts shown here with the accompaniment on the iPad.

- Write a vocal rap that can be performed with this accompaniment.

- Write lyrics and a melody for this piece and sing and/or record them.

- Listen to the remaining voices in the piece (primarily percussion, with a few keyboard sounds). Mark the measures where they play and then improvise substitute parts for them so you can play the entire piece with a small group.

Cultures

The next several songs explore musical cultures from around the world. Included is music from Ireland, Japan, Cuba, Africa, Mexico, Jamaica, Australia, and America.

Ireland: "Old Gray Goose Jig"

ACTIVITY:

This song is from the book's digital fies and is labeled 14-Old_Gray_Goose_Jig.band.

Music from every part of the world is unique, and that is true of this Irish jig, too. It is likely that this traditional Irish dance was often played on the violin or flute. This arrangement has drums, flute, and violin. Like many Irish songs, this one is in $\frac{6}{8}$ meter and has a lilting rhythmic feel.

Performance and activity suggestions:

- See the notes at the beginning of this chapter.

- Experiment with different tempos for this song.

- Describe the characteristics of Irish jigs (lilting, $\frac{6}{8}$, repetition, and so on).

"Sakura"

ACTIVITY:

This song is from the book's digital files and is labeled 15-Sakura.band.

"Sakura" is a Japanese folk song that is known to every schoolchild in the nation. Like most Asian music, it uses a pentatonic scale (a scale with only five notes in the octave). Western popular and art music use seven notes in the scale (eight if you count the octave). Interestingly, a number of well-known American melodies (such as "Amazing Grace" and "Jesus Loves Me") are also pentatonic, although they are often harmonized with the full Western scale. The pentatonic scale used in "Sakura" is the Hirajoshi form (a minor pentatonic scale), so the piece's tone is somewhat darker than most Asian music. Still, the topic of the song is a celebration of the cherry blossoms in spring, so it is not a sad piece.

Performance and activity suggestions:

- Review the notes at the beginning of this chapter.

- Experiment with different sounds for each track of this song.

- Write your own pentatonic song. Use either a major (C–D–E–G–A) or a minor (C–D–E♭–G–A♭) scale.

"Cuban Song"

ACTIVITY:

This song is from the book's digital files and is labeled 16-Cuban_Song.band.

Cuban folk music has a strong Latin influence. This song contains rhythms and instruments common to many Latin songs.

Performance and activity suggestions:

- See the notes at the beginning of this chapter.

- Experiment with different arrangements of the loops used to build this song.

"Drum Complex"

ACTIVITY:

This song is from the book's digital files and is labeled 17-Drum_Complex.band.

In many cultural traditions around the world, music notation is not used. One such tradition is in the drum music of Africa. To stay together, drummers often repeat a 12- or 16-count cycle with performers entering with their instruments on specific counts. Music in this tradition is often layered, so that one instrument at a time enters and establishes its pattern. Other instruments then join. In this recording, the instruments join the group in the pattern.

Performance and activity suggestions:

- See the notes at the beginning of this chapter.

- Play this song slowly to learn it. Perform it at double time for the best musical results.

- Choose a percussion instrument from one of the drum kits and play along with one of the instrument parts.

"La Bamba"

ACTIVITY:

This song is from the book's digital files and is labeled 18-LaBamba.band.

This Latin dance piece is often sung at weddings. Ritchie Valens recorded a popular version based on the original folk tune. His arrangement and recording is protected by copyright, but the original folk song shown is in the public domain.

Performance and activity suggestions:

- Refer to the notes at the beginning of this chapter.

- Record the lyrics to this song using the Spanish and English lyrics.

- Create a custom arrangement, building as much energy as possible into the performance. Use characteristic Latin drums from GarageBand's loops.

Jamaica: "Reggae"

ACTIVITY:

This song is from the book's digital files and is labeled 19-Reggae.band.

Reggae is a style of music with Latin influence that originated in Jamaica and its nearby islands. It is typically characterized by a light sound with carefree lyrics. This version is instrumental only. The off-beats played by the guitar are typical of this music, although often they are played on the beats, but every other one (beats 2 and 4). This song is in a minor key, which is somewhat atypical of the style.

Performance and activity suggestions:

- See the notes at the beginning of this chapter.

- Write lyrics and record yourself singing them. Match the reggae vocal style.

Australia: "Waltzing Matilda"

ACTIVITY:

This song is from the book's digital files and is labeled 20-Matilda.band.

"Waltzing Matilda" is well known in Australia. Virtually every schoolchild is acquainted with it. Although the predominant language of Australia is English, this song contains some vocabulary most English speakers don't know.

Performance and activity suggestions:

- See the notes at the beginning of this chapter.

- Look up the lyrics online and identify each unfamiliar word. Look up the definitions.

- Explain to a friend what the song is about.

Folk Music: English Folk Song with an Appalachian Treatment—"Dueling Yankee Doodle"

ACTIVITY:

This song is from the book's digital files and is labeled 21-Dueling_Yankee_ Doodle.band.

This song is a great example of *theme and variations*. It takes a familiar melody and presents it numerous ways (with different rhythms, melodies, and harmonies). It especially includes a number of phrases of the songs doubled (repeated in "trading" style with the banjo and guitar).

Performance and activity suggestions:

- Refer to the notes at the beginning of this chapter.

- Play this song in two groups, with the banjo and guitar instruments playing their respective parts.

- See the more challenging easy and difficult arrangements of this piece in the online PDF.

- Identify each theme (they generally follow the rehearsal letters) and describe each variation technique used in each section.

"Country Dogs"

ACTIVITY:

This song is from the book's digital files and is labeled 22-Country_Dogs.band.

Notice the use of a guitar-picking style that is common in some early country music. "Country Dogs" is instrumental only.

Performance and activity suggestions:

- See the notes at the beginning of this chapter.

- This song has a simple verse of eight measures and a chorus of eight measures. Copy and paste to expand the song form.

- Write and record lyrics for this song.

- Create a theme-and-variations version of this song.

- Select each track and set the quantization to swing.

Appalachia: "Turkey in the Straw"

ACTIVITY:

This song is from the book's digital files and is labeled 23-Turkey_in_the_Straw.band.

"Turkey in the Straw" is a fiddle tune often used in square dances. Although this version has no lyrics, the traditional lyrics are light and humorous.

Performance and activity suggestions:

- Refer to the notes at the beginning of this chapter.

- Record yourself singing the traditional lyrics. Throw in an occasional "yee haw."

Events

The songs in this section are organized around events that may incorporate music. These include seasonal tunes.

"Birthday"

ACTIVITY:

This song is from the book's digital files and is labeled 24-Birthday.band.

Some claim that the song "Happy Birthday" is protected by copyright law. Others dispute this claim. If it is indeed protected, then many birthday celebrations owe royalties to the copyright owner.

People wishing to steer clear of the controversy may write their own birthday song. You may have heard different versions in restaurants. "Birthday" is a unique birthday greeting with strong syncopation.

Unique features of this song include the use of the Em chord on the first and third phrases, although the song is in C Major. Also, the chromatic harmony on the last two lines contributes to a more dramatic ending.

Performance and activity suggestions:

- See the notes at the beginning of this chapter.

- Mute the solo track and play the melody on an instrument of your choice.

- Mute the vocal track and record yourself singing the melody.

"A Song of Blessing"

ACTIVITY:

This song is from the book's digital files and is labeled 25-Blessings.band.

This piece is an instrumental version of a popular song of blessing. It uses synthesized instruments and builds steadily from start to end.

This song is organized in a verse and chorus form. The first two lines are the verse, and the second two are the chorus. The iPad version of this song is written as a theme and variations, with the entire verse and chorus presented before each variation.

Performance and activity suggestions:

- Open the iPad arrangement and play the melody with the accompaniment.

- Each repetition of the verse and chorus introduces new elements, such as drums and new instruments. Listen to this piece. What devices contribute to the steady building of excitement throughout? How is each variation different?

- Open a different tune and use these techniques to make theme and variations using that song.

A Song of Winter: "Darlin' It's Too Cold" (or "The Whistling Song")

ACTIVITY:

This song is from the book's digital files and is labeled 26-Darlin_Its_Too_Cold.band.

This song contains only two tracks—guitar and a melody, which is whistled.

Performance and activity suggestions:

- See the notes at the beginning of this chapter.

- Delete the melody and record yourself whistling the melody.

- Use GarageBand's guitar effects to add overdrive to the recorded guitar.

A Song of Christmas: "Emmanuel"

ACTIVITY:

This song is from the book's digital files and is labeled 27-Emmanuel.band.

This familiar holiday song originated sometime between the eighth and twelfth centuries. Its melody is modal, meaning that while it sounds minor, some chords are not used the way we would use them in minor songs today. The unexpected chords from centuries ago provide interest for modern ears.

Performance and activity suggestions:

- See the notes at the beginning of this chapter.

- Locate the original lyrics and record yourself singing them. Try to match the original style.

A Song of Christmas: "Jingle Bells" Minor Remix

ACTIVITY:

This song is from the book's digital files and is labeled 28-Jingle_Bells.band.

This version of "Jingle Bells" has an immediately noticeable difference. It is written in a minor key. That gives the song a darker feel, and many parts of the melody are unexpected. Surprises in music are often enjoyable, and this arrangement has several. The song begins with a short introduction and includes several interludes between repetitions of the minor version of the song.

Performance and activity suggestions:

- See the notes at the beginning of this chapter.

- Open the iPad file and play the melody along with the accompaniment.

- Some parts of this arrangement are "eerie." Locate and remove those.

- Copy the song and edit it note by note to make one section major again. (Hint: Change all E-flats to E-natural, A-flats to A-natural, and B-flats to B-natural.)

A Song of Christmas: "Hallelujah"

ACTIVITY:

This song is from the book's digital files and is labeled 29-Hallelujah.band.

Handel's "Hallelujah Chorus" is well known and loved. This iPad arrangement contains instrumental versions of all parts.

Performance and activity suggestions:

- See the notes at the beginning of this chapter.

- Change the sounds of the iPad to make the ensemble sound more natural.

- Find a soprano, an alto, a tenor, and a bass and record them singing their parts with this song.

"Resurrection"

ACTIVITY:

This song is from the book's digital files and is labeled 30-Resurrection.band.

The notation (downloadable from the book's website) has two lines: the melody in the treble clef and a contrapuntal line in the bass clef. The song is organized into two sections: the verse and the chorus. The verse is found in lines 1 and 2 and is unusual in that both phrases end in exactly the same manner. It's more common for two phrases to start the same but end differently, but this song takes the opposite approach. The chorus is found in lines 3 and 4 and has contrasting material, especially in a stronger melodic line in the bass voice. The iPad version is performed with a triumphant tone, and instruments that start loud get louder, building to an even more triumphant climax.

Performance and activity suggestions:

- Review the notes at the beginning of this chapter.

- Listen to this song. Describe the instruments used. Describe the techniques used to build the song.

- Copy this song and paste it at the end of the iPad file. Create a new variation from the copy.

- You can make an effective ensemble from this song with the treble and bass lines, and a GarageBand smart instrument playing chords. Choose instruments that match the tone of the iPad arrangement.

Just for Fun

The songs in this section are hard to classify. They involve some element of celebration.

"Albert the Bluesman"

ACTIVITY:

This song is from the book's digital files and is labeled 31-Albert_the_Blues_ Man.band.

In this song, the influence of tunes such as "Frosty the Snowman" are evident. The accompanying patterns use a similar boom-chuck piano, and the harmonies use similar patterns of accidentals. The lyrics focus on laughing and playing, which are common themes in children's songs. The boom-chuck accompaniment is a common approach to harmonizing songs and was used extensively by composers such as Scott Joplin. Search YouTube for "The Entertainer" or "Maple Leaf Rag" to hear songs that contain similar accompaniments and harmonies but that are very different in style.

Performance and activity suggestions:

- See the notes at the beginning of this chapter.

- This song presents the chorus three times, with instrumental interludes between them. Write and record lyrics to replace the instrumental interludes.

- Turn off the vocal track and sing along with the accompaniment.

- Turn off the drum tracks and replace them with live drums played in GarageBand. Any of the GarageBand drum sounds would work well for this song.

- Turn off the solo guitar tracks and improvise new melodies. The GarageBand overdrive guitar would be a good choice for this song.

- Turn off the piano track and improvise a boom-chuck accompaniment. The GarageBand grand piano would be a great choice for replacing this instrument.

If you have people in your group who can do all of these, then you can perform the piece with no accompaniment.

"Old MacDonald"

ACTIVITY:

This song is from the book's digital files and is labeled 32-Old_McDonald.band.

This familiar children's song makes liberal use of sound effects from the original GarageBand.

Performance and activity suggestions:

- Read the notes at the beginning of this chapter.

- Download additional farm animal sounds to the iPad and create an arrangement that features the sound of specific animals as you sing about them. You can add recordings of farm animal sounds to your iPad's iTunes library and select them in the sampling keyboard or loops for use in a GarageBand for iOS song.

"Everybody Come Around"

ACTIVITY:

This song is from the book's digital files and is labeled 33-Everybody.band.

Numerous songs use the syllable "whoa" much as previous generations may have used the syllable "la." A modern remake of "Deck the Halls" might well have the next phrase as "whoa a, whoa a, whoa, a whoa, whoa, whoa." Often, the "whoa" section is written in an uplifting manner. That is true of this song as well.

Performance and activity suggestions:

- See the notes at the beginning of this chapter.

- This song starts with an eight-measure introduction followed by two times through an eight-measure verse and once through an eight-measure chorus. The song then repeats all of that. Write and record a second verse (or second, third, and fourth verses). Add instruments and more active parts to build energy throughout.

"All Glory, Laud and Honor"

ACTIVITY:

This song is from the book's digital files and is labeled 34-All_Glory_Laud_and_Honor.band.

This triumphant song has four parts. It is the only song written for four voices.

Performance and activity suggestions:

- See the notes at the beginning of this chapter.

- Experiment with different instruments on each voice of this piece.

- Form an iPad ensemble with five members. Each should play a written part, and one should improvise a drum accompaniment.

"Clap Your Hands"

ACTIVITY:

This song is from the book's digital files and is labeled 35-Clap_Your_Hands.band.

"Clap Your Hands" is written in a light, popular style. It includes a verse, chorus, and bridge organization common to most songs on the radio today. The almost universal form of any popular song on the radio today is as follows:

Introduction, verse 1, chorus, verse 2, chorus, bridge, chorus

Sometimes, a section may be repeated (two choruses at the end, for example) or an instrumental may be inserted, but few other variations are common.

Performance and activity suggestions:

- See the notes at the beginning of this chapter.

- Describe the exact form of this piece.

- Write lyrics for the song and record yourself singing them.

"Celebration"

ACTIVITY:

This song is from the book's digital files and is labeled 36-Celebration.band.

The tune is in a light, popular style, similar to the preceding song.

Performance and activity suggestions:

- Review the notes at the beginning of this chapter.

- Describe the form of this piece. Is it the same as the preceding one?

- Write lyrics for this song and record yourself singing them.

"C–F–C–G Activity"

ACTIVITY:

This song is from the book's digital files and is labeled 37-CFCG_Activity.band.

Many piano students learn to play chord progressions that they call *cadences.* Often the first chords they learn are C, F, C, G, C, because these chords are common in many folk, popular, and classical tunes. This song is based on those chords.

Performance and activity suggestions:

- See the notes at the beginning of this chapter.

- Use the features of the smart instruments to create alternative accompaniments for this song.

- Compose and record lyrics for this song.

- Copy and paste to extend the form of this song.

"GB Drum Rondo"

ACTIVITY:

This song is from the book's digital files and is labeled 38-Drum_Rondo.band.

A *rondo* is a classical form in which there are many sections of the music, labeled with letters. The A section is the first, and when there is a new section of contrasting material, we label it B. A rondo uses a recurring A theme, as might be illustrated in this most popular form: ABACABA. Of course, many different rondo schemes are possible, but none is as popular as that one. The *Masterpiece Theatre* tune is a famous rondo. This drum rondo is unique in that the sections are very short. Each theme is two measures long.

Performance and activity suggestions:

- Refer to the notes at the beginning of this chapter.

- Listen to the rondo and see whether you can identify the A section every time it occurs. Make a map of the entire rondo.

- Using only GarageBand loops, create your own rondo in ABACABA form.

"Playing Drums"

ACTIVITY:

This song is from the book's digital files. There are several drum files for Playing Drums that are labeled: 39a-Playing_Drums-Basic_Kit.band, 39b-Playing_Drums-Latin_Kit.band, 39c-Playing_Drums-Rock_Kit.band, 39d-Playing_Drums-Shuffle_Kit.band, 39e-Manual_Drums.band

These drums are for playing.

Performance and activity suggestions:

- See the notes at the beginning of this chapter.

- Use these drums as the foundation for live performances by muting and soloing tracks while others play along. These drums work better in live performance than in jam sessions.

- Play these drums as follows.

  ♦ Start with the basic drums.

  ♦ When you want more energy, add the basic drums—loud.

  ♦ When you want even more, add the ride cymbal to the mix.

- Load a song and record these drums to accompany.

"The One and Only"

ACTIVITY:

This song is from the book's digital files and is labeled 40-The_One_and_Only.band.

This piece uses a chord progression similar to the doo wop chords, but in a style that is more characteristic of contemporary popular music.

Performance and activity suggestions:

- See the notes at the beginning of this chapter.

- Write and record lyrics for this song.

"Palm Pipes"

ACTIVITY:

This song is from the book's digital files and is labeled 41-Palm_Pipes.band.

In Chapter 4 on sampling, we introduced the sound of palm pipes. The Blue Man Group often uses this sound in their performances. This piece uses a very approachable ostinato in the lower voice and a challenging melody in the upper voice. Open this file with your iPad and then open either sample instrument to play with this sound.

Performance and activity suggestions:

- Review the notes at the beginning of this chapter.

- Listen to a Blue Man Group song from YouTube. Use the palm.wav sound to compose a song that sounds like that performance.

Chapter 10: External Devices

GarageBand for iOS recognizes numerous external devices with ease. These devices generally fall into the following categories: MIDI and audio.

There are many manufacturers of MIDI and audio equipment, including those in the following list. It would be impossible to describe all of their products, but the discussion that follows will cover the major categories.

- IK
- Akai
- Alesis
- Allen & Heath
- Apple
- Apogee
- Avid
- Behringer
- DiGiGrid

- Focusrite
- Griffin
- iConnectivity
- Korg
- Line 6
- M-Audio
- PreSonus
- Roland
- Yamaha

Most MIDI and audio devices that can be used with a computer connect through the USB port. The iPad does not have a USB port; however, Apple and a number of third parties make a Camera Connection Kit that provides a USB port for audio and MIDI interfaces. As you might imagine, the Camera Connection Kit also supports video and still-shot cameras. This USB port, however, does not support USB file storage devices, such as external hard drives or flash drives. File transfer onto and off of the iOS device is described in Chapter 8.

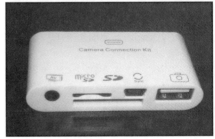

Figure 10.1 Camera Connection Kit 1

Figure 10.2 Camera Connection Kit 2

The Camera Connection Kit comes in separate versions to connect to older and newer iOS devices. The one with 30 pins works with older devices, while the lightning connector is for more recent iOS devices. There are also adapters that will permit 30-pin devices to be used with newer iOS devices, but when adapters require adapters, it's usually time to just buy one more suited for the connection.

You can plug both MIDI and audio interfaces and equipment into the USB port that is available through the Camera Connection Kit.

MIDI Devices

MIDI technology has been included on keyboards and other electronic instruments since the 1980s. GarageBand on the iPad can play notes received through its MIDI input with any of its virtual instruments, and can record MIDI data in any of its songs.

Connecting Your MIDI Instrument to Your iOS Device

Many modern keyboards and drum machines have a USB MIDI output that allows you to plug them directly into the Camera Connection Kit. These MIDI USB devices, however, will only work if they use Apple's Core MIDI technology and if they don't require special software drivers.

If you have a keyboard or other MIDI device that does not have USB MIDI output, you can still use it with the iOS device if it has a MIDI Out port and can be used with a MIDI-to-USB interface like the one in Figure 10.3. In this case, the USB cable from the MIDI interface would plug into the Camera Connection Kit, and the MIDI In cable from the MIDI interface would plug into the keyboard's MIDI Out port. (The signals coming out of the keyboard go into the iOS device.)

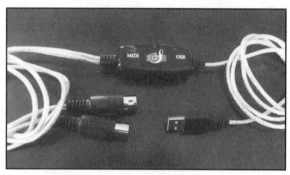

Figure 10.3 MIDI Interface

There is a second cable from the MIDI interface that would normally be used, but GarageBand for iOS cannot send MIDI signals to the keyboard, so you don't need to plug the MIDI Out cable from the MIDI interface into the keyboard's MIDI In port.

If you are using another recording program that can send MIDI signals to an external keyboard (and if your keyboard has sounds and is not just a controller), then you would plug the MIDI Out cable into the keyboard's input.

The MIDI keyboard shown in Figure 10.4 is a controller, so it also needs MIDI communications in the first direction (from keyboard to iOS). Figure 10.5 shows a pedal that plugs into the keyboard. Although, technically, this is external hardware for the keyboard rather than the iOS device, because it is critical to the operation of the keyboard, it is included here. Every MIDI keyboard should have a foot pedal to aid in performance.

Figure 10.4 MIDI Keyboard

Figure 10.5 Keyboard Pedal

To record MIDI in GarageBand, you must be in Instrument view, and the instrument selected must support MIDI input, performance, and recording. The following instruments support MIDI input:

- Keyboard

- Drums

- Smart Guitar (in Note mode)

- Smart Strings (in Note mode)

- Smart Keyboard

These do not:

- Smart Drums

- Audio Recorder

- Guitar Amp

- Inter-Application Communication

When selecting instruments in GarageBand to control through MIDI, the instruments generally perform as expected. Percussion performance, however, requires a little explanation and additional details are found in the section on percussion performance on page 96.

Note: You don't have to do anything special to use MIDI input other than use hardware that uses the Core MIDI drivers. If your MIDI hardware requires custom drivers, there is likely no way to install them on an iOS device. Instead, as described earlier in this chapter, use the MIDI Out port of your keyboard and run that into a newer MIDI interface that uses the standard MIDI drivers.

Note: As mentioned, GarageBand for iOS does not send MIDI signals out of the device. As of this writing, MIDI is for input only. If you need the sound of a specific MIDI device to be recorded, you must record it as audio. (Plug the audio output of the keyboard into an audio interface as described in the audio interface section on page 96.) Other iOS apps *do* support MIDI output—notably Cubasis—and for them you may connect both cables and use a MIDI keyboard that produces sounds also.

There is one other important consideration. If you are using a MIDI keyboard that draws power from the USB port, it may not work—at least, not for long. Obviously, the iPad battery will be quickly drained if it has to drive the electronics in the iPad and in the keyboard. Several solutions are available.

First, a powered USB hub, such as the one shown in Figure 10.6, can provide the electricity for the keyboard and pass signals through to the iOS device. In those cases, plug the keyboard into the USB inputs and plug the output of the USB hub into the Camera Connection Kit.

A second solution is to power the keyboard from batteries if possible. While batteries add an extra layer of inconvenience, it is nice when they're an option.

A third option may be to operate the keyboard with an external power source, if supported. If that is the case, then you can plug the keyboard into a wall outlet

Figure 10.6 Typical powered USB hub with multiple inputs.

for power, and the USB port will be relieved of the duty of providing power for the keyboard.

Finally, there are some third-party Camera Connection Kits that are powered to charge the iOS device, to provide power to the external MIDI device, or both.

Playing GarageBand Percussion Instruments Using MIDI

The GarageBand drum map generally follows the specifications as defined in the General MIDI standard. Many musicians are acquainted with General MIDI from working with percussion sounds on keyboards and drum controllers.

While GarageBand for iOS and for Mac supports only a subset of the General MIDI collection, it does a good job of handling the standard drumset instruments, as shown in Table 10.1. If you need a vibraslap or another unusual percussion instrument in your song, however, the best way to get it may be to record an actual instrument on a digital audio track, or perhaps for additional flexibility, record it using the sampling keyboard.

TABLE 10.1 DRUM MAP FOR CLASSIC ROCK KIT ON GARAGEBAND iOS

MIDI NOTE	GARAGEBAND'S CLASSIC ROCK KIT	GENERAL MIDI DRUM ASSIGNMENTS
C2	Bass Drum (Kick)	Bass Drum
C#2	Side Stick	Side Stick
D2	Low Snare	Acoustic Snare
D#2	Not Assigned	Hand Clap
E2	High Snare	Electric Snare
F2	Floor Tom	Low Floor Tom
F#2	Closed Hi-Hat	Closed Hi-Hat
G2	Not Assigned	High Floor Tom
G#2	Close Hi-Hat (use after A#2)	Pedal Hi-Hat
A2	Low Tom	Low Tom
A#2	Open Hi-Hat	Open Hi-Hat
B2	Not Assigned	Low-Mid Tom
C3	High Tom	Hi-Mid Tom
C#3	Crash Cymbal	Crash Cymbal
D3	Not Assigned	High Tom
D#3	Ride Cymbal	Ride Cymbal
E3	Not Assigned	Chinese Cymbal
F3	Ride Dome	Ride Bell

Note: Other drum kits in GarageBand have variations on this mapping but are similar.

Audio Interfaces

These devices connect an audio device, such as a microphone, to the iPad. The advantage of this is that an appropriate interface allows you to record with a fully professional microphone.

These devices are divided into several subcategories, including those that support dynamic microphones, condenser microphones, and line inputs (such as from guitars or keyboards) and those that mix various signals into the computer. These devices could also be categorized according to how they input their signal into the iOS device, with input into the 30-pin or lightning adapter preferred, but input through the headphone jack is also a possibility.

While the microphone that comes with the iOS device is quite good, it is sometimes possible to use alternatives to good effect. These microphones plug directly into the headphone jack of the iOS device. The iRig external mic in Figure 10.7 provides a handheld mic that may be used to move closer to a sound source than the iOS device. The iRig MIC Cast shown in Figure 10.8 also plugs into the iOS device, but it provides a condenser input more suited to interviews around a table.

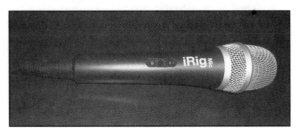

Figure 10.7 iRig external mic.

Figure 10.8 iRig MIC Cast.

The pair of TASCAM stereo condenser microphones shown in Figure 10.9 is built to be plugged directly into the 30-pin port of the older-style iOS devices. These same stereo microphones were used on a highly respected class of handheld recorders by this manufacturer.

If you want to use your own professional-quality microphones, you may need a device like the iRig PRE shown in Figure 10.10, which permits a standard XLR microphone cable to be connected through it to an iOS device. This device includes a preamplifier and may be used with dynamic and condenser microphones, including those that require phantom power (see Figures 10.11 and 10.12).

Figure 10.9 TASCAM stereo condenser mic.

Figure 10.11 Shure SM58 dynamic mic.

Figure 10.12 Shure KSM27 condenser mic.

Figure 10.10 iRig PRE for connecting dynamic and condenser mics.

Some instruments (guitars, basses, and keyboards) have a 1/4-inch output. You can use an adapter like the one shown in Figure 10.13 to pass the signal from a guitar (plug into the port on the left) to the iPad (plug into the iPad using the cable on the right).

Figure 10.13 iRig 1/4-inch line-in adapater.

Audio interfaces make up the final category of devices that you can use to connect audio equipment to the iPad. These provide the best quality. The audio interface shown in Figures 10.14 and 10.15 connects through the USB port of the Camera Connection Kit into the iOS device, and the inputs on the back of the device support a number of input types, including XLR microphones, 1/4-inch inputs, RCA inputs, and so on. As long as the audio interface doesn't require any custom drivers, it should work on the iOS device.

Figure 10.14 TASCAM audio interface (front).   Figure 10.15 TASCAM audio interface (rear).

Because these devices have a longstanding historical use with computers, they are a mature technology with numerous features. There are audio interfaces that support one, two, four, eight, or more inputs of various types (two being most common for iOS devices). There are devices with preamplifiers, monitoring systems, and phantom power. And because this is a mature technology, the price is not excessively high. The biggest change for manufacturers of these products is that now they are often designing models that have a cable that plugs directly into the iOS device instead of going through the Camera Connection Kit.

Chapter 11: iPad Jam Sessions

Jam Sessions on the iPad permit up to four performers to play together using any combination of GarageBand instruments. A key feature is that you can synchronize smart instruments that generate automatic accompaniments so that they play together. You don't have to use auto-accompanying instruments or features, but if you do, this is the best way to ensure the beats will align in the ensemble.

Additionally, you can have GarageBand designate one person as the bandleader, who can collect everyone's performance into one recording when the performance is finished.

Starting a Jam Session

To initiate Jam Sessions, up to four iPads must be on the same network. The network can be a traditional 80211 (A, B, G, N) wireless network, or it can be a Bluetooth connection initiated by the bandleader. To create the Jam Session, all the iPads join the same network (wireless on and connected to the same router, with passwords if necessary) or turn on Bluetooth (in the Jam Session window).

One member will serve as the bandleader. That person will go to the Jam Session menu and select Create Session. The Jam Session menu will expand to show the following options.

- **Bandleader Control.** If this is on, the play, rewind, and record buttons will work only from the bandleader's iOS device. If it is turned off, any member of the band can press play, rewind, or record.

- **Auto-Collect Recordings.** If this is on, after a recording session, the musical files are automatically copied to the bandleader's iOS device. By default, they are copied with the Mute switch on. The bandleader must unmute any track once it is copied to his or her device. If Auto-Collect Recordings is not turned on, there is still a Collect Recordings button that copies the band members' files to the bandleader's device. One advantage of having Auto-Collect turned on is that it sends each band member's work to the bandleader after every recording. An advantage of having it turned off is that you can play through the piece several times and have band members select the track that is best. They can delete the poor tracks before the bandleader selects the Collect Recordings menu option.

Joining a Jam Session

To participate in a Jam Session, after the bandleader has created the session, the other band members must go to the Jam Session menu. There, they will see the session listed (and any other active sessions on their network) and can tap the desired session to join (see Figure 11.1).

Figure 11.1 Band members will find the active sessions listed on this screen.

Figure 11.2 The bandleader can tap Stop Session.

The bandleader can tap Stop Session, and band members can tap Leave Session (see Figure 11.2). If the bandleader's device times out (shuts down), the session is automatically finished. The bandleader will have to start the session again, and members will have to join again.

Jam Session Tips

A notable limitation of Jam Sessions is that only four instruments can be played together at the same time. The easiest workaround is to have the bandleader do two recording sessions, one after the other, perhaps one with one set of members and another with a second set of members. The tracks that have been collected to the bandleader's station can be turned on to play during recording, so the remaining band members can hear the tracks recorded to that point.

It may be possible for iPad instrumentalists to play along with the Jam Session (not with smart instruments) to record their own tracks, send them to the bandleader, and have the bandleader copy and paste the tracks into the recording. However, the number of steps and details that must be solved to have success with this approach makes the process prohibitively complex. It is far better to record in two different passes.

The collaborative process made possible through GarageBand's Jam Sessions feature is exceptional. Students work and perform together, or the process will not work. When they are successful, they have a product that demonstrates that accomplishment. Music teachers have often used performance in small chamber ensembles to accomplish musical goals. These same benefits are realized through the Jam Session technology.

Sharing a Jam Session

To share the final project with other students, the easiest way is for the bandleader to email a mixed-down version to students from the GarageBand Song List view. Alternatively, the bandleader can use iTunes file sharing to send the GarageBand file to his or her laptop or desktop computer, where it can be emailed to band members, who can then open the file in their version of GarageBand for iOS for editing or keep it as a memento.

One other file-sharing option is enabled by Jam Sessions. If each band member creates a session (in turn), and only the original bandleader joins, the new bandleader can copy the files to his device by manually choosing Collect from the Jam Session menu.

NOTE: The original band leader should not create a new session, even if prompted, until each member has copied the files to their new session.

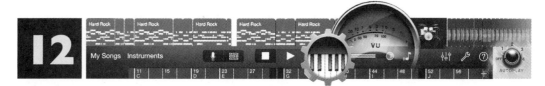

Chapter 12: Things Teachers and Group Leaders Need to Know

There are some things that teachers and group leaders need to know about using an iOS device in the classroom, such as how to project the screen from the device, how to send the device's sound to a sound system, how to control a computer from the device and vice versa, how to sync an iOS device with a computer, and how to get information onto and off of the device. This chapter addresses these topics.

Projecting the iOS Device Screen

There are several approaches to projecting the image from an iPad to a computer screen or monitor. The various methods with their pros and cons are described below.

Projecting with Cables

The least expensive and most reliable way to connect an iOS device to a monitor for projection is through a cable available from Apple. There are, however, several important considerations.

First, you must be aware of whether your iPad or iOS device supports video out. You must have an iPad 2 or later or an iPhone 4s or later. While some older devices support video output from some apps, using equipment older than that will not produce consistently satisfying results. Teachers will generally want to mirror the screen of their iOS device to the projector, and that requires an iPad 2 or later, or an iPhone 4s or later.

Figure 12.1 Apple 30-pin connector cable.

Next, it is important to purchase a connector that fits your iOS device. Apple used a 30-pin connector cable with iPads through the fourth generation and the iPhone 4s (see Figure 12.1). Starting with the iPhone 5, Apple switched to a 10-pin lightning connector (see Figure 12.2). The video adapter should fit the iOS device with which it will be used.

Finally, you must consider the input of the device to which you are connecting for projection. Fortunately, today almost every projector and large-screen display device supports VGA input, and many support HDMI. Apple makes adapters for iOS devices that output either VGA or HDMI. It is important to purchase the version required by your projector (if it doesn't support both).

Figure 12.2 Apple 10-pin lightning connector.

Because you will be using a cable to connect your iOS device to your computer, you'll need a cable that is long enough to comfortably reach the work area where the iOS device will be used. Because the cable physically connects to the device, you'll lose some portability. Also, you may experience reduced battery life on the device when using projection because there is greater drain on the battery and because the projector plugs into the port normally used for charging the device (although Apple's HDMI cable has a charging option). It pays to start most presentations well charged and to get into the habit of recharging between presentations.

So, by way of summary, to connect an iOS device to a projector or monitor, you need the following:

- An iPad that supports video mirroring (iPad 2 and later, iPhone 4s and later)

- An adapter that fits into your iPad (either 30-pin or 10-pin)

- An adapter that plugs into your monitor or projector (either VGA or HDMI)

- A cable that's long enough to reach your workspace

About Sound

The projection discussed so far is for video only. To play sounds from your iOS device in the classroom, the solution is much easier. Purchase a good set of computer speakers and plug an 1/8-inch cable from the speakers into the iOS device's headphone port. Turn up the volume on your iOS device and on the speaker system, and you should be ready to go. Because you're plugged in for video projection anyway, another cable plugged into your iOS device is no additional burden. Of course, you don't have to use computer speakers. Any sound-reinforcement system that will receive an input from an 1/8-inch cable will do.

Projecting with Apple TV

Apple has a solution that permits wireless transmission of your iOS screen to a projector. For this, you will need a second- or third-generation Apple TV, a compatible iOS device, and a compatible monitor.

As before, the first step is ensuring that your iOS device is compatible with the Apple TV. To use Apple TV, you will need one of the following iOS devices: iPhone 4s or later, iPad 2 or later, iPad mini or later, iPad Touch (fifth generation or later). As before, if your system doesn't meet these criteria, it's best to consider updating that equipment or looking for another solution.

Next, it is important to ensure that your projector or monitor is compatible with the second- or third-generation Apple TV. This could be an issue because the video outputs of the Apple TV are only HDMI (no VGA). Because many projectors do not support HDMI, you could easily end up in a situation where you do not have a projector that would support the output of your Apple TV.

This is especially true if you travel with your iOS device to conference centers. There are converter boxes that will change a VGA signal to HDMI, and you could use them to bridge the gap between the Apple TV and older projectors and monitors. However, these converters are typically about the same price as the Apple TV, so it's not quite as easy as just buying an inexpensive adapter. Don't forget to pack the converter if you will be traveling with your Apple TV.

A few more considerations apply to the Apple TV: The Apple TV device and the iOS device must be connected to the same WiFi network, and that network should not be one that is overly restricted. The iOS device must be running iOS 7 or higher with video mirroring turned on. Additional information may be obtained by searching Apple's support site if needed.

So, by way of summary, to connect an iPad to a projector or monitor through an Apple TV, you need the following:

- An iOS device that supports second- or third-generation Apple TV (iPhone 4s or later, iPad 2 or later, iPad mini or later, or iPad Touch fifth generation or later)

- A second- or third-generation Apple TV

- A projector or monitor that supports HDMI input, or possibly a box that converts HDMI to VGA or to another input supported by your current projector or monitor

More About Sound

The solution we discussed earlier, where you plug an 1/8-inch cable from a good set of computer speakers into the iOS device, will work in this circumstance also. See the earlier "About Sound" section for details.

You may also have some success sending the audio from your iOS device to Apple TV. Apple TV should theoretically have two options for sending audio to a set of speakers: through the HDMI connection and through an optical audio output port on the Apple TV box. If neither of these options works (depending on the monitor, projector, or audio system with which they are used), be certain that your Apple TV has the most recent firmware updates and that your iOS device is also updated to the latest iOS.

If all else fails and plugging into a good set of computer speakers is too restrictive, AirPlay provides another set of wireless audio options. The AirPlay technology has been around for several years now, and it should work, even if you're using the cable-and-adapter projection discussed earlier.

From your iOS device, choose an output for your audio. If there are any AirPlay devices in the area where you use your iPad, select those devices for your output. AirPlay devices include the following:

- AirPort Express with a traditional RCA audio output

- Apple TV with HDMI and optical audio outputs

- Any number of third-party AirPlay speakers, which receive, amplify, and play the sounds with no further connections

The icon in Figure 12.3 is often available on your iPad when AirPlay devices can be selected.

Figure 12.3
AirPlay icon.

Other Methods for Projecting Wirelessly from Your iOS Device

A number of apps run concurrently on your Mac and iOS devices and permit the iOS screen to transmit to the computer for projection. Unfortunately, many of these applications impose some restrictions. For example, some require that both the iOS device and the computer be on the same WiFi network, which is not always possible. Also, as with Apple TV, the WiFi network should not be one that is overly managed, for example, with a large number of blocked ports.

To try one of these applications, download and start with AirServer, Reflector, or X-Mirage. A free version of each is available to test the network, computer, projector, and iPad. If one of these works, it may be a more practical and affordable wireless solution than Apple TV. Just purchase the app, configure it to work with the computer, and wirelessly send audio and video to your Mac, which handles the projection and playback of sound as it normally would.

Viewing Your Mac Screen on Your iOS Device

A number of apps support sharing the screen from your computer with the iPad or other iOS device. Start with TeamViewer and see whether it meets your needs. TeamViewer works in this manner: Install and run the app on your computer and on your iOS device. Enter your computer ID and password into the iOS device, and the computer screen will appear on the iPad in just seconds.

Setup is quick and operation is reliable. Both devices must have an Internet connection. However, they do not have to be on the same network or in the same room. TeamViewer can connect devices that are hundreds or thousands of miles away, as long as there is a reliable Internet connection to both.

In addition to viewing the screen of the other device, TeamViewer supports other features, such as remote control of another device, audio communications, and file sharing, depending on the system on which it is operated.

TeamViewer is free for personal use, but commercial (and educational) use requires the purchase of a license. If all you are doing is sharing a screen, the price may seem expensive, but the additional features of TeamViewer and its reliable operation make it a good value.

Controlling Your Mac Using Your iOS Device

There is a class of computer programs that permit the iPad to control your Mac remotely through the Internet. A software called iTeleport is one such program. You can control the computer remotely from your iPad for any number of tasks that a computer can normally do, but that an iPad cannot.

iTeleport works like this: Install and run iTeleport on your iOS device. Install and run iTeleport Connect on your computer (Windows or Mac). On both machines, log in using your Gmail credentials. iTeleport on your iOS device will locate your computer and permit you to take control of it from your iOS device.

Syncing an iOS Device and a Computer

Apple has designed iOS devices to sync nicely with laptop and desktop computers. Normally, a teacher's photos, music, and other media are stored most permanently on a desktop or laptop computer, and copies are made to any iOS devices paired with that computer, based on the settings for that device in iTunes and the amount of storage on the iOS device. If the iOS device is not large enough to hold the entire music, photo, movie, and book collection from the desktop or laptop, the content to be synced will have to be managed in iTunes.

In iTunes on the Mac, click on the iOS device, then click each of the tabs at the top of the screen to select the files that will be synced. If the iOS device and computer are not synced, it is difficult to copy many files back and forth from the iOS device and the computer. Teachers should not resist this important step. The process is simple. Just plug your iOS device into the computer, and when prompted as to whether you want to sync with the computer, answer Yes.

One problem that iOS users sometimes encounter is when they use multiple computers. While the rules may be changing in this area, and people do find ways to work around these restrictions, normally it is best to sync each iOS device to a single master computer. It's okay to sync multiple iOS devices to the same computer, but it's sometimes a problem to sync an iOS device to multiple computers. Each computer overwrites the previous one's music, photos, movies, and so on.

The good news, however, is that for GarageBand files, you can copy files that are not synced through Apple's iTunes file sharing. So, syncing takes care of a number of issues, but with iTunes file sharing, you can work with iOS devices and computers that are not synced with one another.

Facilitating Effective Use of GarageBand for iOS

While it is an easy thing to overlook, one problem that teachers must solve is how to connect the iOS device to the Internet. A related problem is how to enable students' email on the iOS device. While it is possible to work without any Internet access, it should be clear to the teacher that the prospect of connecting 25 iPads to a teacher computer to collect student projects is a logistical nightmare. Multiply that by a number of classes, and the problem escalates.

A couple of technologies offer some possibilities for making this process more friendly. If all the iOS devices can be set up on the same iCloud account with enough storage, and students take care in naming their projects, then the process of collecting and sharing files is greatly simplified.

Another possibility is the AirDrop technology, which permits file sharing. As of this writing, this technology is still evolving, but it offers promise. Apps such as GoodReader and iFile enable some easier sharing of files over the network, but again, you must give some attention to configuring accounts so that solutions are possible. Also, these particular solutions may not work as well with GarageBand because of the difficulty of getting useful files to and from GarageBand.

At least one school district has worked with Google to create Gmail accounts for all their students. The accounts are restricted in a manner that protects the students' privacy but open in a way that permits students to email or share their projects with teachers. The advantages of this approach are that students can quickly share their GarageBand projects on YouTube (operated by Google), and students can use email to receive iOS GarageBand files from the teacher, like those from this book. This approach and its variations deserve consideration.

For districts where this is not possible, it is very likely that the IT department will have to be involved in creating a solution that enables the best use of the devices, especially for sharing information with teachers. The IT department could consider ways to provide iPads with email addresses that are not the students' normal emails, or they could consider ways to permit students to use their school email on the devices. It may also be possible for all student iPads to share the same iCloud account. (While this provides a number of solutions, it creates a few problems with security and privacy.)

There is one other file-sharing option worth mentioning for the sake of being thorough. This final option has only limited use. An easy way to get GarageBand projects from one iPad to another is by connecting through a Jam Session. When the files are collected, the bandleader receives all band-member tracks that are in the currently open song. If a teacher were to establish a new Jam Session, and one student with a complete project were to join it, the teacher could manually select Collect, and the student's work would be copied to the teacher's open song. Again, this file-sharing option works well for individual students, but it doesn't have the efficiency required for working with classes with large numbers of students.

Installing Apps on iOS Devices

Syncing multiple iOS devices to a single computer allows you to install and manage a common set of apps on many devices. The advantage of this approach is that you can make a backup of each iOS device when syncing with the computer.

Another technique for installing apps from one account on multiple devices is to enter the login information for the Apple account on the iOS device, then visit the App Store. Any apps purchased with that account can then be downloaded to that device. Teachers will find these two techniques useful because they often have to manage apps on a large number of iOS devices.

Capturing Screens in iOS

Teachers who actively use iOS devices with their students might want to prepare handouts showing the screens that students may encounter in completing an assignment, to guide the students through selecting the correct options. To capture the screen on an iOS device, display the desired screen and then hold the Home and Sleep/Wake buttons simultaneously. You'll hear a camera click, indicating that the iOS device captured the screen. You'll find the image in the photos of the Camera app, and you can email it from the screen where it is displayed. (Tap on the box with an arrow coming from it.) You can also send the picture in any number of other ways (through syncing, through a photo stream, by downloading from Image Capture, and so on).

All of these methods work equally well, but email is an easy way to quickly send one photo. Once the photo shows up in the email on the computer, right-click it and copy and paste it into a word processor, or right-click it and save it to a location where it can be used. If you have multiple screen-capture images, one of the other methods may be more efficient.

Printing from an iOS Device

iOS devices cannot connect to printers by cable, but they can connect by WiFi. Addtionally, you cannot install custom printer drivers on iOS devices, but the devices can print to printers that support AirPrint. Fortunately, a growing number of modern printers do.

To use AirPrint, make certain you are on the same WiFi network as a printer that supports AirPrint. From the iOS app, tap the Share button (a box with an arrow pointing out of it, or a rounded arrow pointing up). In the dialog box that appears, select your printer and the number of copies you want, and tap Print.

Creating PDF files from an iOS Device

Creating PDF files from iOS devices is an area that is constantly changing. There isn't yet the same level of development or standardization as on laptops or desktops, where creating PDFs from any document is built into the Apple operating system. One app that may be used to create PDFs is Save2PDF, but teachers are encouraged to search Apple's App store for new developments.

The issues addressed in this chapter are not ones that are typically a great concern to individual users. Teachers, however, will need this information to more effectively use their iPads and other iOS devices in the classroom.

Chapter 13: Additional GarageBand Activities for the Classroom

The following list of activities is provided for teachers who wish to develop further lessons for GarageBand for iOS, as well as for their students. The ideas given here are in a concise form; teachers can expand them as needed. Likewise, students can self-direct through these activities if they are interested.

1. Create an audio soundscape (which could be any group of synth pads).

2. Record a program for a radio broadcast. Write the dialogue for the drama. Write a score for the musical background.

3. Create a musical intro and outro for a television program. Imagine writing something for the evening news as it starts and ends, or for your favorite sitcom.

4. Record a soundtrack for a familiar television episode or a silent movie.

5. Record a story and add sound effects from GarageBand.

6. Compose a song with loops only. (Learn about form, repetition, and contrast.)

    A. Two sections (A and B)

    B. Contrasting range, rhythm, melody

7. Compose a percussion piece in rondo style using the automatic drum machine.

8. Write a loop-based jingle for an imaginary product and record a melody for it.

9. Create a loop-based song describing animals (like Saint-Saens' "Carnival of the Animals").

10. Create a loop-based song in a distinctly 1940s swing combo style.

11. Create a loop-based song in a distinctly 1950s doo wop style.

12. Create a loop-based song in a distinctly 1960s rock style.

13. Create a loop-based song in a distinctly 1970s classic rock style.

14. Create a loop-based song in a distinctly 1980s keyboard disco/dance and/or hip-hop style.

15. Create a loop-based song in a distinctly 1990s ballad style.

16. Create a loop-based song in a distinctly 2000s techno style.

17. Create a loop-based song in a distinctly 2010s style.

18. Record a round of a song, such as "Are You Sleeping?," and copy and paste it into multiple tracks.

19. Practice a piano piece and record it on an iOS device using MIDI.

20. Open a song of your choice from those in the book. Create a new audio track, and every four measures say "Oh yeah" or something similar and record it.

21. Add a drum build every four measures to a song of your choice from those in the book. Mute existing drums if necessary.

22. Add a repeat and fade ending to a song of your choice from those in the book.

23. Add expressions (dynamics) to a song of your choice from those in the book.

24. Add expressions (tempo changes).

25. Replace the melody track of a song of your choice (from those in the book) with your voice singing the melody.

26. Add a harmony part with your voice to a song of your choice.

27. Add drums to a song of your choice.

28. Create new guitar tracks for a song of your choice.

29. Delete an existing melody, and write and record a new melody and lyrics for a song of your choice.

30. Write a new song by recording an accompaniment with smart instruments and then recording a melody and original lyrics.

31. Play and record the 12-bar blues chord progression using one of GarageBand's smart instruments; then compose and record a melody with original lyrics.

32. Play and record the 12-bar blues chord progression using one of GarageBand's smart instruments; then improvise and record a scat melody.

33. Play and record the doo wop chord progression using one of GarageBand's smart instruments; then compose and record a melody with original lyrics.

34. Create an accompaniment for a melody copied from one of the GarageBand songs in the book.

35. Create a rap to be performed over one of the hip-hop, dance, or techno songs from those in the book.

36. Rehearse and prepare every voice of a simple *a cappella* song. Record each track into GarageBand for iOS.

37. Record yourself singing a song. Listen to it and critique your performance.

38. Write and record a new pop song. Include all parts using loops, digital audio, or MIDI recordings.

39. Write and record a new classical song.

40. Write and record a new round.

41. Write and record a theme and a variation.

42. Remix a set of given tracks from one of the songs in a new and different way.

43. Participate in a Jam Session and record the team effort as a song.

44. Technical skills:

A. Import a MIDI track.

B. Import a digital audio track.

C. Add effects to an existing track (reverb, compression, echo, and so on).

D. Quantize rhythms.

E. Send audio and/or video output to AirPlay speakers and/or Apple TV.

F. Export GarageBand song to:

i. Email

ii. iTunes

iii. AirDrop

iv. Facebook

v. YouTube

vi. SoundCloud

vii. GarageBand for Mac

viii. Logic

ix. Ringtones

x. iCloud

G. Use GarageBand with Audiobus (See Chapter 15) and other music apps.

H. Merge tracks.

I. Edit regions.

i. Edit MIDI (regions, notes, and so on).

ii. Cut, copy, paste, duplicate, split, and delete MIDI and digital audio.

iii. Trim a region.

iv. Loop a region.

v. Join regions.

vi. Snap to grid (on/off).

J. Manage regions (A, B, length).

K. Manage master effects (echo, reverb).

L. Turn the metronome on/off.

M. Turn count-in on/off.

N. Set the project tempo, key, and time signature.

O. Create a fade-out.

P. Play music in the background.

Q. Expand the mixer.

R. Monitor and manage levels, mute, solo, and pan tracks.

S. Save songs, open songs, and manage songs.

T. Enter note mode and play instruments using MIDI input.

U. Record audio using external hardware for input.

V. Layer (merge) recording of tracks.

Apple Tutorials

Apple has done a great job of documenting its iOS apps. Both teachers and students may benefit from reading and watching the materials.

GarageBand for Mac

- www.apple.com/mac/garageband

- help.apple.com/garageband

GarageBand for iOS

- www.apple.com/ios/garageband

- help.apple.com/garageband/ipad/2.0

Chapter 14: Inter-Application Communications

GarageBand for iOS has an extensive collection of instruments, including smart instruments that enable easy but impressive performance of musical materials. GarageBand also has a strong collection of effects (echo, reverb, and so on) that you can apply to various tracks. Even with all of that, wonderfully creative developers have written additional musical apps with features not found in GarageBand. Fortunately, starting with version 2, GarageBand supports inter-application communication, which permits third-party apps to seamlessly integrate with GarageBand.

Two classes of apps can use GarageBand's inter-application communications: instruments and effects.

Inter-Application Instruments

While Apple's Smart Drums do an outstanding job, many people enjoy performing with and recording the drum patterns that are available in programs like FunkBox. Because FunkBox supports inter-app communications, it can be used as an instrument input for a GarageBand inter-app communication track.

Here's how to do it:

1. Create an inter-app track in GarageBand for iOS. (Tap the + button at the bottom of the tracks and select an inter-app communication track (see Figure 14.1).

2. When the screen permitting you to select instruments or effects appears, click instruments and select FunkBox (or another instrument you would like to use as an input). The only instrument apps available on this screen are those that support inter-app communications (see Figure 14.2). If you don't see any icons, you may not have any compatible apps. A number of free apps are available, so a basic search should yield some choices for you. After you make this selection, you will notice a plug icon in the upper-left corner of the screen that lets you change the settings (select a different instrument app) if desired.

3. Switch to the desired app by tapping its icon in GarageBand.

4. Tap Record on that app's transport (in Figure 14.3, in the upper-left corner). Note that you will see a GarageBand icon by the transport that is not normally there, because inter-app communication is active.

Figure 14.1 GarageBand instrument selection: Inter-App Audio Apps.

Figure 14.2 GarageBand inter-app communication: Instruments.

Figure 14.3 FunkBox drum machine.

5. You will hear a count-off (if turned on in GarageBand) and any background tracks recorded in GarageBand. Play the desired musical lines using that app. Play musically and in time with the GarageBand metronome and/or accompaniment.

6. When you're finished, tap Stop on that app's transport (usually a square button or the word "Stop").

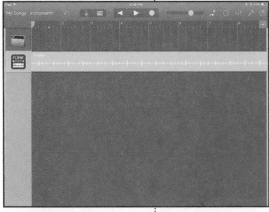

Figure 14.4 Recorded track in GarageBand.

7. Switch back to GarageBand by tapping its icon on the app's transport. Notice that the audio from that app was recorded into a track in GarageBand (see Figure 14.4). Note: If the instrument app plays music (as FunkBox does), it may be aware of the tempo in GarageBand and match it, which makes things much easier. If the instrument app does not sync correctly with GarageBand's tempo, you may have to manually set the tempos of the two apps to the same value beforehand and align the recorded track with the beat in GarageBand afterward. FunkBox automatically detects the tempo and syncs the beat.

This seamless level of connecting compatible apps with GarageBand expands the instrumental choices available for recording in GarageBand.

Inter-Application Effects

Again, you can apply GarageBand for iOS effects, such as echo and reverb, to each track. Creative developers, however, have created stand-alone effect apps, such as AUFX:Dub, that provide reverb, detuning, equalization, tremolo, and other effects. Using inter-app communication, you can record these effects with a digital audio track. Many of these effects are not available in GarageBand alone, so inter-app communication allows GarageBand to include features that are not native to it.

Here's how to do it:

Figure 14.5 Inter-app communication: Effects.

1. Create an inter-app track in GarageBand for iOS. (Tap the + button at the bottom of the tracks and select an inter-application communication track.)

2. When the screen permitting you to select instruments or effects appears, tap Effects and select AUFX:DUB (or another app you want to use as an effect); see Figure 14.5. The only effect apps available on this screen are those that support inter-app communications. If you don't see any icons, you may not have any compatible apps. You can use a number of free apps, so searching should yield some choices.

3. After you make this selection, you will notice a plug icon in the upper-left corner of the screen that lets you change the settings (select a different effect app) if desired (see Figure 14.6).

4. Switch to the app being used to create effects by tapping its icon in GarageBand, and adjust its settings as desired (just the right amount of reverb, equalization, and so on; see Figure 14.7).

5. Tap Record on that app's transport. Note that you will see a GarageBand icon by the transport because inter-app communication is active. You will hear a count-off (if turned on in GarageBand) and any background tracks recorded in GarageBand.

6. Record the desired musical lines. Unless you've added an instrument that can be played (you can add both instruments and effects), the music recorded will be through GarageBand's input (probably the built-in microphone). Play musically and in time with the GarageBand metronome and/ or accompaniment. Note: If you added an instrument, you should initiate the recording session from the instrument app's transport, rather than from the effect app's transport.

7. When you're finished, tap Stop on that app's transport.

8. Switch back to GarageBand by tapping its icon on that app's transport. Notice that the audio with effects from that app was recorded into a track in GarageBand.

Again, this seamless level of connecting compatible apps with GarageBand expands the choices available for recording effects in GarageBand. Although effects apps often implement the items mentioned (reverb, equalization, and so on), a number of effects applications have been written that expand the types and quality of guitar amplifiers and effects pedals available in GarageBand for iOS.

The current use of inter-application communications will certainly expand with time. It's easy to imagine that instrument apps could be written that would play standard MIDI files in sync with GarageBand's metronome. As of this writing, GarageBand cannot officially import Standard MIDI files, but if an inter-app communications instrument app plays them, GarageBand can record them.

A promising app that is still in the early stages of development is Musk MIDI Player. This program can play MIDI files, but tempos do not automatically sync, and the program has to have a General MIDI sound font installed to work well. Also, it's easy to imagine that effects apps will be written that will permit dynamic or panning automations to be recorded in real time.

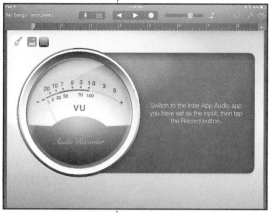

Figure 14.6 Instrument performance and preferences.

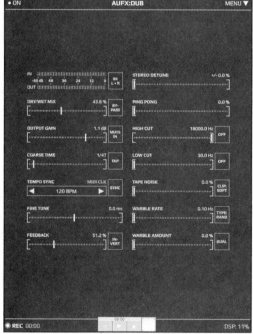

Figure 14.7 AUFX:DUB effects app.

Chapter 15: Audiobus

A technology that slightly preceded inter-application communication but is very similar is implemented in the popular Audiobus application. This application runs in the background on an iOS device and supports three types of devices: inputs, effects, and outputs.

The inputs are equivalent to the instruments in GarageBand's inter-app communication. The effects in both are the same. The outputs in GarageBand's inter-app communication are always assumed to be an audio track in GarageBand. With Audiobus, outputs can be directed to other recording software, such as MultiTrack DAW, Cubasis, Auria, Loopy, and others.

Why Audiobus?

So, if inter-app communication and Audiobus do nearly the same thing, why do we need Audiobus? First, Audiobus supports recording (outputs) by software other than GarageBand. Many excellent recording apps are available, and people will favor one over the other for various reasons. Audiobus's support of additional outputs is welcome.

Second, although this may change, as of this writing, more apps are compatible with Audiobus. Because GarageBand is also compatible with Audiobus, you can use the two together to achieve a level of seamless operation that is remarkable for apps developed by completely different companies.

Third, although there is some additional cost for this feature, Audiobus supports multi-routing, in which, for example, you can use more than one instrument as an input or as an effect (depending on the memory and speed of your iOS device).

Of the three types of devices supported by Audiobus (inputs, effects, and outputs), you can use GarageBand for iOS only as an input or an output. As an output, it functions exactly as it did in inter-app communications (as a place to record music). As an input, it plays music that can be recorded by other recording software.

The great strength of Audiobus is that it enables you to use features not normally available in GarageBand. Although inter-app communication is free with GarageBand, you may face some costs to acquire the third-party apps it relies on. Audiobus has more features; however, although it is affordable, it does require a purchase in the App Store (and additional features, such as multi-routing, require in-app purchase).

Using Audiobus

To use Audiobus, follow these steps:

1. Launch Audiobus. A screen with three cells will appear. From top to bottom (or left to right, depending on your screen orientation), the cells represent inputs, effects, and outputs, as shown in Figure 15.1.

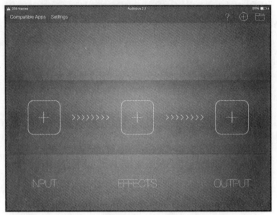

Figure 15.1 Audiobus App: main screen.

2. Tap each cell to set the desired options (see Figures 15.2 through 15.4).

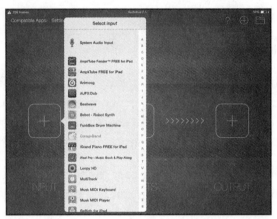

Figure 15.2 Inputs.

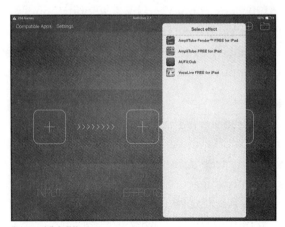

Figure 15.3 Effects.

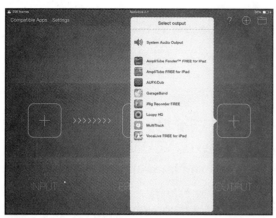

Figure 15.4 Outputs.

3. The icon for each selected app appears in the cell, and each app should be launched and any desired settings entered before recording (see Figure 15.5). You'll need to repeat this step for all apps used by Audiobus for this recording. Note: It is essential that you manually set the tempos for any apps to the same setting because, as of this writing, tempo syncing does not appear to be supported. This also means that once a recording is made, you may have to adjust the placement of the recording to align more precisely with the beat.

Figure 15.5 Multi-routing configuration.

4. When you're in any app other than Audiobus, there will be a small side menu on the screen with the icons of the other applications in the setup. The app that serves as an output will have a transport in the side menu, from which you can rewind, record, and play the track (see Figure 15.6).

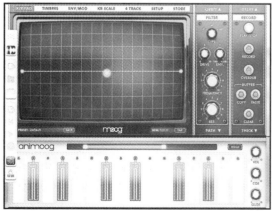

Figure 15.6 Animoog synthesizer.

5. Normally, the last steps in recording using Audiobus are to:

  A. Switch to the app selected as the input.

  B. Press record in the Audiobus output transport from that screen.

  C. Play the input instrument as desired.

  D. When finished, press Stop in the Audiobus output transport from that screen.

Both Audiobus and GarageBand inter-application communications are implemented on a low level of system operation and, consequently, both perform very well. Both systems, however, are subject to occasional technical glitches—for example, when an application doesn't have enough RAM to launch or enough iOS processing power to perform as expected. With these technologies, you might obtain better performance by turning off notifications, alarms, WiFi, and cellular services (if applicable) and clearing the memory of any apps that are not a part of the session. (In current iOS systems, double-tap the Home button and swipe away any unused apps.)

Chapter 16: Automations

As musical pieces unfold, there are often changes in the dynamics that accompany each part of the song. For example, the following dynamic scheme is commonly used in popular music:

- Intro (loud)

- Verse (soft)

- Chorus (loud)

- Verse (soft)

- Chorus (loud)

- Bridge: Repeat four times – (1) soft, (2) medium soft, (3) medium loud, (4) loud

- Chorus (loud)

- Repeat and fade out

Normally, performers will make these adjustments themselves, but sometimes it falls on the producer or sound engineer. Most recording software for desktop and laptop computers allows you to automate volume controls for each track and for the song overall (the master track). You can also automate other controls, such as panning and reverb, in professional software.

Dynamic "Automations" in GarageBand for iOS

GarageBand for iOS does not permit you to create or edit automations after a track has been recorded. For this reason, it may be worthwhile to send each GarageBand for iOS project to a laptop or desktop for some dynamic touchups.

If you prefer to work exclusively in GarageBand for iOS or if you have a situation where using a laptop or desktop is not possible, the following technique may be useful.

Consider a circumstance where a novice group performs an entire song at more or less the same dynamic level. If the sounds can be balanced throughout (using the volume sliders for each track), then you might be able to merge the tracks and then duplicate the track at three or four dynamic levels. By splitting the merged track at the various sections (verse, chorus, and so on) and moving each section into a track at the desired dynamic level, you can achieve an automated effect. See Figure 16.1.

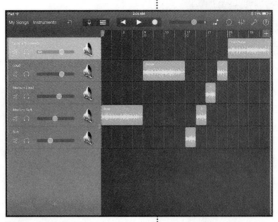

Figure 16.1 Dynamic "automations" in GarageBand for iOS.

Figure 16.1 demonstrates how to accomplish dynamic variations on the level of the "master" track, but you can apply the same principle to individual tracks too, with some limitations on how many tracks are available.

One effect usually accomplished through automations that GarageBand for iOS does well is the fade-out. This technique was explained in Chapter 5.

As mentioned, GarageBand for Mac has greater support for automations, and it is easy to send the GarageBand for iOS source files through iTunes file sharing to GarageBand for Mac for further editing. Although some iOS recording apps *do* support automations (Cubasis being the primary one), there is no easy way to send GarageBand source files to them. You can send each GarageBand track as a digital audio file to Cubasis and then add automations. However, because of the time-consuming nature of this transfer, it would be easier to do the entire recording project in Cubasis from the start, or find a Mac with GarageBand on which to add the automations.

Automations During and After Recording MIDI

GarageBand records some automation data when it is recording MIDI. It records movements of the pitch bend and modulation wheels, as well as the use of the sustain pedal. Volume changes with the instrument master slider are not recorded, but velocity instructions (on velocity-sensitive keyboards) are. The ability to alter velocity gives you a great deal of control over the volume of the song.

After GarageBand has recorded these items, you can do some editing of pedal marks and velocity in GarageBand for iOS, but no apparent method of editing pitch bend or modulation is clear. If you transfer a GarageBand for iOS song to a Mac by iTunes file sharing, you can add all of these items and additional post-production automations.

Chapter 17: Other Things You Can Do with Your iPad

GarageBand for the iPad is a substantial program that offers an extensive set of features. The iPad, however, supports a number of additional musical apps that may be used in conjunction with, or independently of, GarageBand. The Technology Institute for Music Educators (TI:ME – _http://www.ti-me.org_) identifies six categories of music technology with which music educators should be acquainted. TI:ME calls these technology strategies:

1. Notation

2. Production

3. Instruments

4. Instructional Software

5. Multimedia

6. Systems and Production

iPad apps support each of these categories. The chapter below is organized according to TI:ME's technology strategies, but beginning and ending with subcategories of number six.

Utilities

iOS devices support a host of practical apps. There are tuners, metronomes, drum machines, loop devices, effects processors, and more. Whatever the need, it seems there's an app for it. One such app is the Peterson iStroboSoft instrument tuner (Figure 17.1).

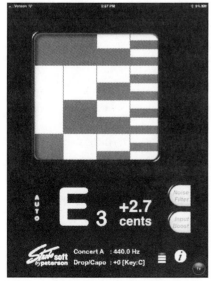

Figure 17.1 Peterson iStroboSoft for the iPad.

Notation

Year after year, notation software has proven to be one of the most useful music technologies. With it, teachers can create custom arrangements for their students, create warm-ups and worksheets, generate project notation while playing scores, and more. On desktop and laptop computers, Finale and Sibelius have a large share of the notation market. Both Finale and Sibelius have readers and players for their files on iOS devices. While several companies are working on notation programs for iOS devices, as of this writing, neither Finale nor Sibelius has released an iOS program you can use to create or edit notation.

The best option as of this writing is Notion. Users of any previous notation program will feel comfortable with its interface and will be pleasantly surprised by its features. Notion is a notation program for writing, playing, printing, and publishing music. You can import and export MusicXML files from Sibelius or Finale. See the following demonstrations:

- Create score: *www.youtube.com/watch?v=rtRUk46qHac*

- Enter notes: *www.youtube.com/watch?v=riUZEIIazrA*

Also, check out Finale SongBook, a free app for playing and viewing Finale scores (.mus files), shown in Figure 17.2, and Avid Scorch, a free app for playing and viewing Sibelius scores (.sib files), shown in Figure 17.3.

Figure 17.2 Finale SongBook for iPad by MakeMusic.

Figure 17.3 Scorch for iPad by Avid.

Production

Music teachers can record their performing ensembles and classes for several useful educational purposes. This technology enables teachers to critique their ensemble's performances and help their students hear what went well and what didn't. Teachers can record student auditions and create assessment artifacts that document student progress.

GarageBand, shown in Figure 17.4, is by far the premier iOS music-production app. However, many others are also useful. MultiTrack DAW has some features not found in GarageBand, especially in terms of effects. Auria offer a full set of professional features, including up to 48 tracks. The Cubasis music production system is probably the most developed at this point, and it specifically addresses many of GarageBand's limitations (including the inability to import MIDI, the inability to control external MIDI devices, and the inability to create and edit automations in post-production).

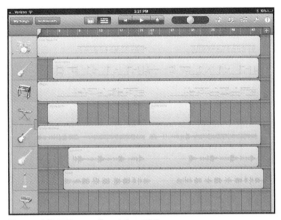

Figure 17.4 GarageBand for iOS.

You can use many of these applications concurrently with GarageBand to enhance the recording process. The Audiobus app and Apple's new inter-app communication make it convenient for these apps to exchange information with GarageBand.

Virtual and Electronic Instruments

Electronic instruments are an essential component of any lab used to teach music. Traditional electronic instruments, such as keyboards and drums, are popular, but virtual instruments are gaining ground.

Increasingly, recorded music includes virtual instruments like those that come with GarageBand and other production programs. Plus, additional virtual instruments independent of GarageBand are being developed. When you select and correctly configure the proper virtual instruments, your musical output will be significantly improved.

Audiobus and GarageBand's inter-app communication permit these virtual instruments to work together with GarageBand and other iOS DAWs. Figure 17.5 shows Moog's Animoog Synthesizer, which enables sounds that are not otherwise possible in GarageBand. Using Audiobus, you can perform and record those sounds in GarageBand.

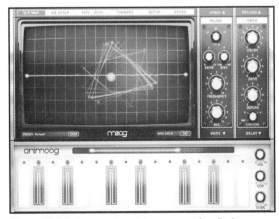

Figure 17.5 Animoog virtual instrument for iPad.

Instructional Software

Every serious student of music is interested in improving his or her understanding of music. Many instructional software applications can help you develop musical skills and insights. iOS apps such as Theory Lessons by musictheory.net, shown in Figure 17.6, do an excellent job of explaining complex concepts in a simple manner.

Figure 17.6 Theory Lessons for the iPad by musictheory.net.

- **Everyday Looper.** A looping program for live performance and improvisation. See the demonstrations at _www.youtube.com/watch?v=FWmhk8sxMy0 and www.youtube.com/watch?v=4kk6F-tgm7g._

- **Rhythm Cat.** A program for practicing rhythms.

- **Treble Cat.** A program for practicing treble clef notes.

- **Rhythm Lab.** A program for practicing rhythms.

- **VidRhythm.** An app for creating songs with dynamic video effects—highly entertaining.

- **MadPad.** An app for creating dynamic video projects.

- **Bebot.** A singing robot that you can control interactively.

- **Soundrop.** A compositional tool that creates music similar to the pioneering electronic music piece "Dripsody."

Multimedia

Musicians and teachers have two primary needs in multimedia: to show presentations, and to create and edit them. Creating and editing presentations also requires the development of various multimedia elements (text, graphics, audio, video). Once developed, multimedia presentations may be distributed through blogs and social media, and used to promote programs. The iPad is capable of all of these tasks.

The most familiar multimedia presentations are often created in a program such as Microsoft PowerPoint. While there is no currently available PowerPoint for the iPad, Apple does offer Keynote, which can play PowerPoint presentations, and which can create and develop its own uniqe slide shows.

Other multimedia presentations take the form of movies. Apple's iMovie is an excellent program for developing video presentations.

Many iPad apps, for example, GarageBand or notation software, are capable of presenting multimedia experiences as their screens are displayed. Because these dedicated apps work directly with musical materials, their presentations often far exceed what is possible in more general software such as PowerPoint or Keynote.

Creating the text, graphic, audio, and video elements for presentations is easily accomplished using an iPad. Any of the apps mentioned above in the production section can be used to develop multimedia. Some of the most common multimedia apps are described below.

- **Keynote.** An app for creating slideshows with text, pictures, sounds, and video and pro-level transitions.

- **GarageBand.** An app for developing audio for many purposes.

- **iMovie.** An app for creating and editing video, and for adding and customizing the various elements including text, photos, and audio.

People often use iOS devices as recording devices for programs and concerts. You can take the footage you've recorded, edit it on your iOS device, and send it to YouTube using iMovie for iOS. One quick tip: Be sure to turn the iOS device to landscape orientation, so that the long side is parallel with the horizon. All modern screens are in this proportion, and the video you record will be much more useful with this orientation.

Figure 17.7 iMovie for iOS.

Built-In Software

While music teachers often gravitate toward musical apps, some of the more practical apps extend the function of iOS devices. The following basic apps that come with an iOS device can be useful for music teachers and students:

- **Safari.** Find and bookmark instructional websites that work on the iPad.

- **Mail.** Establish a community of like-minded musicians and stay in touch.

- **Photos.** Take a photo of every musical instrument you own, in an artistic manner. Share the photos with colleagues.

- **iTunes.** Buy a song from the iTunes Music Store and share it with classmates or students.

- **YouTube.** Identify useful YouTube Videos for learning about music and share them with classmates or students.

- **Camera.** Take photos or video of a concert you attend. Share the pictures or video. Record one song as a movie. Edit it with iMovie and share it.

Apple Software

The following Apple software can provide useful activities for music teachers and students:

- **iBooks.** Find, download, and install useful iBooks for teachers and students.

- **Pages.** Write a musical essay—for example, on the life of a composer—and include pictures.

- **Numbers.** Import your school music budget into Numbers.

- **Keynote.** Create a musical presentation—for example on the history of music technology—and include pictures.

Chapter 18: Unofficial File Transfer Options

Officially, Apple says it's impossible to send a MIDI file to GarageBand for iOS, and to send a GarageBand for Mac file to GarageBand for iOS. Apple recommends converting the MIDI file and GarageBand for Mac file to digital audio files and sending those to GarageBand for iOS, either through iTunes or iTunes file sharing. If this approach meets your needs, it's safe and secure, and it's far easier than everything that follows.

The disadvantage to Apple's approach is that the MIDI and track editing features are then no longer available. If the MIDI file or GarageBand for Mac file is a finished product, this isn't a big concern. However, if your project requires you to do further MIDI or track editing in GarageBand for iOS, then you may try an unofficial technique for taking the files to GarageBand.

Before reading further, be advised that moving into unchartered territory like this means that some results may not be completely satisfactory, and future updates could cause these approaches to cease to work. You may want to reread the first paragraph and skip to the next chapter.

However, many people have original MIDI files that could be used in GarageBand for iOS, and by keeping them in MIDI format, the instrument with which they are played can be reassigned, and the files can be further developed. This chapter provides instruction on transfering MIDI files to GarageBand for iOS in the hopes that it will be useful for such time as it is still functional.

Sending a GarageBand for Mac File to GarageBand for iOS

The information that follows shows you a workaround that permits you to send both MIDI files and GarageBand for Mac files to GarageBand for iOS. The steps listed here are the steps for attempting to send a MIDI file, but the same steps should work in both cases.

By way of a quick overview, the process is to open a Standard MIDI file in GarageBand for Mac, save it as a GarageBand for Mac file, edit the file type information, and send the file through Apple iTunes files sharing to the iOS device. If all goes well, the MIDI file will appear on your iPad, and you can continue to edit it there. For example, you can reassign voices and use the iPad's MIDI editing features.

Here are the details:

1. Begin with a Standard MIDI file. Any would do well, but you'll obtain the best results with MIDI files that need to play a single instrument, such as piano.

2. Open GarageBand for Mac and drag the MIDI file into the gray area where loops are normally added.

3. Assign the instruments for each MIDI track in GarageBand to instruments that are supported in GarageBand for iOS. There is currently no published documentation of these details from Apple. When in doubt, assign the track to piano. You can reassign the tracks (to some degree) later in GarageBand for iOS.

4. Here's an extra step that may or may not be necessary; you can try skipping all of Step 4 if you wish. What this step will do is create temporary freeze files (digital audio tracks) of each track in the song and save them in the Media folder of the GarageBand package. (More information about packages in a moment.) If the MIDI copy is unsatisfactory, this is the fastest way to convert each MIDI file to a separate track.

    A. From the Track menu of GarageBand for Mac, choose Show Track Locks.

    B. Lock each track.

    C. Press Play and wait until each track is locked.

5. Here's yet another step that may or may not be necessary. Go to the File menu in GarageBand for Mac and choose Save As. In the dialog box that appears, select the Archive Project checkbox. This step saves real instrument Apple Loops so that the song can more easily be taken to another computer for additional work. While this may not have any effect on GarageBand for iOS at this point, it may be useful in the future. There are no further optional steps in the process.

6. Save this file on your Mac and edit it as follows. This is the most challenging part. If you can do this, you've got it made!

    A. Right-click the GarageBand file and choose Show Package Contents. GarageBand files are not really files. They are a special type of folder called a *package*, which contains the song data.

    B. Open the file entitled projectData in a text editor, such as TextEdit, and change it as follows:

        i. Find the string indicating the system and change it as follows:
        <string>ios</string>
        Note: It may say "macos." Change that to "ios."

        ii. Find the string indicating the machine and change it as follows:
        <string>iPad2,3</string>
        Note: It may say "x86_64." Change that to "iPad2,3."

        iii. Save this file.

    C. You must do the same thing in one additional file. Find the file metadata.plist, probably in the Output folder.

        i. As before, change the system to "ios."

        ii. As before change the machine to "iPad2,3."
        Note: The data may not be located together as it was in the previous file.

        iii. Save this file.

    D. That's the hard part! Yea!

7. Using iTunes file sharing, send this file to GarageBand for iOS. From the Song List view, tap the + button and choose Copy from iTunes File Sharing. Find the song and open it.

The song should appear to have come over nicely. At this point, it may appear that you have achieved complete success, because the song in GarageBand for iOS will appear to match exactly the form of the song in GarageBand for Mac.

This is the point where you may experience additional limitations of GarageBand for iOS. It may not be able to assign these MIDI tracks to the sounds of smart instruments, such as guitar, bass, strings, or drums. GarageBand for iOS believes these tracks are to be played by GarageBand's Keyboard instrument. The strong track-typing rules in GarageBand prevent the movement of this MIDI data to smart instrument tracks with some of the better sounds.

The good news is that GarageBand's Keyboard instrument supports a large number of sounds (see the "Instruments Supported by GarageBand's Keyboard Instrument" sidebar on page 132) and that you can use many of those instruments' controls to customize them to sound more like the desired instruments.

The good news doesn't stop there! You can also move this MIDI data to a GarageBand for iOS sampler track. See Chapter 4 for more information about how to use it to sound more like real acoustic instruments.

In the future, you might be able to move this MIDI data onto smart tracks. That would give a much stronger performance of much of the MIDI data that you can import into GarageBand for iOS using this technique.

For now, you must check all MIDI tracks and reassign them to instruments that are available in GarageBand for iOS. Specifically, you'll probably have to delete drum tracks and re-create them from scratch in GarageBand for iOS. Fortunately, GarageBand for iOS has excellent existing drum loops and an excellent smart drummer instrument for new drum tracks.

INSTRUMENTS SUPPORTED BY GARAGEBAND'S KEYBOARD INSTRUMENT

Keyboards
Grand Piano, Classical Grand, Electric Piano, Whirly, Soul Organ, Classic Rock Organ, Heavy Metal Organ, and Smooth Clavier

Classics
Evolving Colors, Samurai Strings, Soft Analog, Spectrum Echo, Electric Marimba, Harmonic Sequence, Neon Koto, and Fifth Element

Bass
Retro Bass, Eighties Mixtape, Exoplanet, Hip-Hop Sub Bass, Sabertooth, Car Horn Bass, Classic Synth Bass, and Massive Polygon

Leads
Vintage Lead, Fifties Sci Fi, Hyper Dance, Light Cycle, Reverse Engineering, Warp Lead, Simple Lead, and Inharmonic Lead

Pads
Chill Pad, Ethereal Rhythm, Moonrise, Warming Waves, Dark Matter, Hollywood Strings, Day Spa, and Fuel Cells

FX
Arcade Synth, Pulsar Wind, Hacksaw Bass, Grid Bass, Metallic Bass, Whirlybird, Autofocus, and Suspense Bass

Chapter 19: Accounts You May Need

iCloud

iCloud is a free cloud computing service by Apple that backs up select information from your computer (bookmarks, contacts, and so on). If you have Pages, you can use iCloud to save documents from Pages so that iOS devices and computers can share documents. If you have an Apple ID for purchasing songs on iTunes, you should use it. Your iPad and other IOS devices work best with one account. If you do not have an Apple ID, you can create a new account at www.icloud.com. See this site if you have questions: _support.apple.com/kb/HT4436_.

YouTube

YouTube is a cloud-based computing service for saving and sharing videos. You can use your existing account or create a new one at www.youtube.com. If you have a Gmail account, you can log into YouTube with that. (Google owns both Gmail and YouTube.)

SoundCloud

SoundCloud is a cloud-based computing service for saving and sharing audio recordings. It permits listeners to make comments on a song as it plays, which is excellent for critiquing student work, adding lyrics, or just letting the composer know how you feel about his or her music. You can use your existing account or create a new one at www.soundcloud.com.

Amazon

Amazon is a service for purchasing books and other goods. The Amazon Reader, the Kindle, lets you have instant access to available textbooks on your computer or iOS device (or on Kindle devices you purchase from Amazon). You can use your existing account or create a new account at www.amazon.com.

Dropbox

Dropbox is a cloud-based service for saving and sharing files. You can use your existing account or create a new one at www.dropbox.com.

Box

Box is a cloud-based service for saving and sharing files. You can use your existing account or create a new one at www.box.net.

Google Drive

Google Drive is a cloud-based service for saving and sharing files. You can use your existing Gmail account or create a new one at www.google.com.

Appendix A: Features of GarageBand for Mac and GarageBand for iOS

These features will come and go with new versions of GarageBand for Mac and GarageBand for iOS. This chart is a snapshot of the general capabilities at the time of this writing.

	GARAGEBAND FOR MAC	GARAGEBAND FOR IOS
Records digital audio	Yes	Yes
With built-in microphone	Yes	Yes
With external interface (for pro mics)	Yes	Yes
Sample rate supported	96k	44.1k
Sample depth supported	32 bits	16 bits
Supports multiple tracks	Up to the limits of the CPU	Early versions for iOS were limited to 8 tracks, but recent versions support 16 to 32 tracks, depending on the iOS CPU.
Imports and exports audio file types	Yes	Yes
WAV	Yes	Yes
AIF	Yes	Yes
M4A	Yes	Yes
AAC	Yes	Yes
MP3	Yes	Yes
Records MIDI data performed by the user from onscreen virtual instruments	Yes	Yes
Records MIDI data performed by the user from external hardware instruments	Yes (requires MIDI interface or MIDI device with USB output)	Yes (requires MIDI interface or MIDI device with USB output *and* the Apple Camera Connection Kit)
Imports MIDI files	Yes	No
Exports MIDI files	No	No
Records MIDI controllers, such as pedals, pitch bend, modulation	Yes	Yes
Edits MIDI data	Yes	Yes
Bubble view	Yes	Yes
Score view	Yes	No
Edits MIDI controllers	Yes	No
Records automations in live performance (velocity, pitch bend, modulation, pedal)	Yes	Yes (does not record volume, panning, echo, reverb)

Plays automations	Yes	Yes
Can create and edit automations after recording	Yes	No (although there is a fadeout feature, and velocity can be edited)
Has loops	Yes, various numbers of loops depending on the version of GarageBand and the installation of additional software	Yes, a subset of the loops available on GarageBand for the Mac, about 250 as of this writing
Can add effects to audio and MIDI tracks	Yes	Yes
Echo	Yes	Yes
Reverb	Yes	Yes
Compression	Yes	Limited (through inter-application communications and third-party apps such as Audiobus during recording)
EQ	Yes	Yes (through inter-app communication and third-party apps)
Manual pitch correction	Limited	No
Automatic pitch correction	Yes	Yes (through inter-app communication and third-party apps)
Manual rhythm correction	Tedious	Tedious
Automatic rhythm correction	Yes	No
Other effects	Yes (Apple AU)	Yes (through inter-app communication and third-party apps)
Can add effects to master tracks (echo, reverb)	Yes	Yes
Has smart instruments	No	Yes
Smart instruments generate accompaniment for custom chord progressions	No	Yes
Has piano samples	Yes	Yes
Has guitar samples	Yes	Yes
Has bass samples	Yes	Yes
Has string samples	Yes	Yes
Has orchestral instrument samples	Some, but not all	No, but programmable synthesizers can come close
Has programmable sampler instrument	Yes (AU sampler)	Yes, limited
Has programmable synthesizers	No	Yes, limited
Supports General MIDI	No, you must convert General MIDI tracks to audio and import.	Limited (through inter-app communication and third-party apps)

Note: Logic Pro answers Yes to all of these.

Appendix B: Apple Help for GarageBand and Other iPad Apps

While this book provide's a thorough introduction to GarageBand on the iPad, Apple's support resources are excellent. The pages below are highly recommended. Searching Apple's support site may yield additional information.

Note: Websites sometimes change names or links become inactive, so check the Alfred Website (*www.alfred.com/LearningGarageBand*) for the latest sources for this information.

Apple iOS Apps Support: *www.apple.com/support/ios*

GarageBand for iPad: *help.apple.com/GarageBand/ipad/1.4/index.html*

iMovie for iOS: *www.apple.com/support/ios/imovie*

iPhoto for iOS: *www.apple.com/support/ios/iphoto*

Pages for iOS: *www.apple.com/support/ios/pages*

Keynote for iOS: *www.apple.com/support/ios/keynote*

Numbers for iOS: *www.apple.com/support/ios/numbers*

iTunes U: *www.apple.com/support/ios/itunes-u*

iBooks: *www.apple.com/support/ios/ibooks*

Podcasts: *www.apple.com/support/ios/podcasts*